HEAVY SPIRITUAL PLAYERS *and others who have slipped in uninvited weigh in on Poe Ballantine's enormously entertaining collection of reputedly factual tales*:

This book appears to be more about beer and striking out with women than theological issues. However, I'm convinced that this honest quest, this clear-eyed and blasted view from the gutter, might very well be a crumb in the vast crystalline matrix of the New World Order. —DR. EDWARD VARGA SAGE
Professor of Divinity
Holy Mother of God University

Ravishing work, my son. Voluptuously heartbreaking.
—THOMAS AQUINAS

By grace, through faith, they offed my head in 65, but I'm still here as you see, a Pharisee, a tortured wanderer, like this man Ballantine, by grace through faith, as to all those who wait, and shirk not the light of truth. —ST. PAUL THE APOSTLE

My soul yearns to know this most entangled enigma. I confess to Thee, O Lord, that I really have no idea what Poe Ballantine is talking about. —ST. AUGUSTINE

Anyplace around here I might wash my hands?
—PONTIUS PILATE

How about *501 Minutes to Lunch?* —BARABBAS

More, of course... ☞

OK, so I edited the Bible as you know it, and I was a pagan emperor and all that, but when my Franks and I marched outnumbered under the Christian standard and whipped those Goth mercenaries all the way to the Hellespont, Rome saw another glorious millennium. *In hoc signo vinces.* Remember also: Istanbul was Constantinople. Now it's Istanbul, not Constantinople. Been a long time gone, Constantinople. Now it's Turkish delight on a moonlit night. —CONSTANTINE THE GREAT

We recommend brazen manipulation of Christian iconography. Look what it did for Madonna, and she's not even a real blonde! —SHAMELESS AMERICAN ENTERTAINMENT MACHINE

I resent that remark. The concept of Christianity, much less its iconography, did not exist in my time. And I was never once in my life a blonde, though I do admit to one experiment with henna. —THE MADONNA

We weren't talking to you. Come back and see us when you've got a single on the charts.
—SHAMELESS AMERICAN ENTERTAINMENT MACHINE

Oh, you bore me, you're all so boring. —SATAN

These authors have no idea what a pain in the ass it is filing titles that begin with numbers. —MATT PLIES
Annie Bloom's Books

Copyright ©2007
Poe Ballantine

Library of Congress
Cataloging-in-Publication Data

Ballantine, Poe, 1955–
501 minutes to Christ/
Poe Ballantine.
–1st ed.
p. cm.
ISBN 0-9766311-9-9

I. Title.
II. Title: Five hundred and one
minutes to Christ.

[PS3602.A599A612 2007]
813'.6–DC22
2006100717

Hawthorne Books
& Literary Arts

9   1221 SW 10th Avenue
8   Suite 408
7   Portland, OR 97205
6   hawthornebooks.com
5   *Form*:
4   Pinch, Portland, OR
3
2   *Printed* in China
1   through Print Vision

Set in Paperback.

First Hawthorne
Edition, 2007

All of the essays in this
collection originally
appeared, in one form
or another, in the *Sun*.

To Rhonda Berry Wine and A.W. Snee

ACKNOWLEDGMENTS to Machete Woman, Kato the Cha Cha Champion, and One Adam Twelve McIsaac, the man who makes even strangers want to read me. And Whirly the One-Eyed Squirrel.

ALSO BY POE BALLANTINE:

Things I Like About America
God Clobbers Us All
Decline of the Lawrence Welk Empire

501 Minutes to Christ

Personal Essays
Poe Ballantine

 HAWTHORNE BOOKS & LITERARY ARTS
Portland, Oregon | MMVII

501 MINUTES TO CHRIST

World of Trouble

THE PLACE WHERE YOU GAVE PLASMA LOOKED LIKE IT
had recently been a small grocery store. I had never given blood
or plasma before and had no appreciation for the difference. All
I knew was that you got eight bucks, which was also the going
rate for a full day's labor through Manpower.

A woman with a white smock and immaculately sculpted
hair stood behind a glass case full of baloney sandwiches and
candy bars. I imagined she was happy to see me and my young
blood, not old wino blood. She seemed to have a slight vampire
curl in her smile. I answered her questions: I was eighteen. I was
not a heroin addict. I was presently unemployed. I had no current address. I'd bought these useless boots at an army-surplus
store. The jacket too. I signed a form, and she led me to an
examining table and told me everything would be all right. The
tissue paper crackled as I climbed aboard. There were two
other men reclining on tables, bundles of gauze taped to their
arms, tubes running into dark bottles.

"We're going to draw a pint of blood," the woman explained,
as if I were a keg of Irish stout. "Spin it on a centrifuge,
remove the plasma, return the blood solids to your body, then
we'll repeat the process. It won't take more than an hour."

She smiled and made a vein stand out by cutting off the
circulation in my left arm with a rubber tourniquet. A vein
swelled. She produced not a needle but a pipe, razor sharp, big
around as a pencil and chamfered at the end like the mouthpiece

of a clarinet or the stake you'd drive into Dracula's heart. I didn't believe she would stick anything that big into me. I'll bleed to death, I thought. The blood in my swollen vein will splash the ceiling.

"Ball your fist," she ordered. Then she punched the "needle" in: pain-meat-slice-burn, followed quickly by a deep dull ache that spread to my hand. The blood sped up the tube, my dark life spinning away.

"You've got good-looking blood," she said.

Who but a ghoul would say a thing like that? And we're going to do this twice? How much can I spare? I thought, skinny boy who never ate.

The woman flicked her nail at the filling bottle and asked me where I was from. She had a motherly air despite the vampire curl and film actress hair. I explained that I had recently set out from San Diego, California, to make my fortune. I was going to New York City, where I planned to earn passage on a steamer to France, but I had gotten sidetracked: robbed in Houston and kicked off the trains in San Antonio, a city that also treated me to a pair of tickets for hitchhiking and sleeping on the freeway. A few days earlier my backpack and sleeping bag had been stolen, so I was stuck in New Orleans for a while.

She wanted to know why I was clear down here if I was headed to New York, and I told her I had thought it would be warmer along the southern route, and that I had heard people talking about this thing called Mardi Gras all along the way and thought I might have a look at it, though it had turned out to be just parades and drinking, and I had quickly lost interest.

She looked sympathetic, but her expression said she had heard this story many times before, and soon she had to flit off and check on one of the donors across the way.

I watched my vessel fill. If they removed all my blood, I wondered, replaced it with someone else's, would I still be me? Seven years before, Christiaan Bernard, a South African surgeon, had given a dying patient another man's heart without any apparent personality change. The me in me was pretty deep then, deeper than the blood, the marrow, the heart. If you took out my brain, however, then I wouldn't have these thoughts. And I'd probably have the sense not to be lying on this table with a steel pipe in my arm. I began thinking about sex. Then my fantasies switched to potato chips. I hankered for salt. I was losing salt. I would die not of blood loss but of salt loss. I'll buy salted peanuts when I'm done here, I declared to myself, and red wine, good Concord grape wine blessed by a rabbi, to restore my cells. I dreamed of peanuts and Concord wine. The room began to turn. My head felt the size of an orange.

A grinning white-faced kid entered the room. He looked a little like me, hawk nosed and pimply, with a shapeless haircut and a busted zither of chin whiskers; no character, seasoning, or experience, but bigger than I was by about three inches and fifty pounds. He looked first at me, then at the tube running from my arm into the glass bottle, and he fainted straight over, buckled and twirled into a heap on the tiles. A man in a lab coat scurried out from the back to help him up and back outside.

The woman in the white smock glanced over. "Happens a lot," she said to me. "Especially the big guys." She unhooked my bottle and held it like a newborn, shining and warm. In five minutes she was back with a bag of blood solids.

"Mine?" I said.

"Yours."

"Sure?"

She smiled. "I'm sure."

She hooked the bag to the pole and let my blood drain back. Those cold blood solids may have been my own substance, but, God, they felt like the sticky fingers of the dead crawling back into my arm.

"We'll do this one more time," she said. "Then we'll have you out of here."

I STAGGERED OUT of the storefront plasma joint feeling light as a feather and clutching my free baloney sandwich, blood money folded into my front pocket. I walked for a few disoriented blocks, the sky bright. Finally I stopped, unwrapped the sandwich, and ate. White sheets hanging from a rooftop clothesline snapped in the breeze like flags. I saw a reflection in a bar window: thin, pale, and unkempt in my laughable army-surplus outfit. A trolley rattled by dinging its bell. Off in the distance the behemoth jungle gym they called the Superdome was going up in all its iron trigonometric splendor. The sidewalk, lifted by a tree root, heaved up in front of me like a wave. A man in the sun-blue light of a phone booth leaned over, hand clamped to his ear, as a cement truck shuddered by. A pair of graying flower children weighed down with backpacks turned into a restaurant.

I drifted to my hangout, Jackson Square, a fenced-in park in the French Quarter along the Mississippi River, where the cops left me alone and I could sleep on the grass in the sun. I had finished my baloney sandwich and was still hungry, but also very drowsy. I thought I might take a nap before starting the usual evening scrounge. The winos in their stocking caps played cards under the banana trees across the way. Most of those who hung out in the square fell into one of five categories: lazy, crazy, drug addicted, alcoholic, or criminal. (I hadn't met a true hobo yet, one who voluntarily went without a home.) Still these park dwellers mostly helped me. They told me where the soup lines were, and who was handing out free what. I learned about the mission and Manpower, a temporary labor service. It was the winos who informed me about giving plasma. They also warned me about sleepers getting knifed in the parks at night, which was one reason—not having a sleeping bag to keep me warm anymore was another—that I walked the streets most nights. The night before, I had walked four or five hours, then spent the coldest part of the early morning on the American side drinking nickel coffee at the Hummingbird Café, where I could beat the pinball machine with fair consistency.

My restless night, combined with the plasma loss, now had me exhausted, and I was dozing off when Jules strolled up. He was a pear-shaped kid with short hair parted in the middle like an English grocer from the 1920s. He stood there with his arms hanging, as if he were waiting for someone to tell him the shipment of cantaloupe had arrived. Jules took care of his wealthy aunt, who had polio. He had never worked, and it looked as if he might never have to. Every day he wore a different brand-new sweater; today it was turquoise with chips of Matisse floating across his chest. Some people like to play pinball in their leisure time, or read paperback Westerns, or drink MD 20/20 under the banana trees. Jules liked to hang with street people. I imagine his life was dull, and he lived vicariously through us. He knew all the regulars. "Hey Jimmie! Hey Maxie! Hey Sailor!" he called, as if he were walking into a neighborhood bar. Most of the down-and-outers regarded him as a chump, and the minute he appeared through the gates he was descended upon. But he cheerfully dug down and seemed to have enough spare change for all.

I never asked Jules for money. I was too proud to beg. And anyway, I was only temporarily living on the street. Soon I would save up enough money, the weather would warm, and I would turn north to fortune.

"You look kind of pale today," Jules observed, arms folded across the Matisse sweater. "You OK?"

I told him all about giving plasma, sparing no detail. I made it seem as if I had been doing it every week for years. He listened, saucer-eyed. He thought of me as some sort of accomplished vagabond who enjoyed scraping along the bottom of the city, and I couldn't help but encourage that perception. The fact is, Jules and I were about the same age and had about the same amount of world experience: which is to say, none. The only difference was I had left the safe sterility of the suburbs a month before and, through the simple act of sticking my thumb out on a freeway entrance ramp and using poor judgment ever since, had made for myself a world of trouble. Still, a world of trouble was the recipe for my transformation from a bland child into a seasoned adult, which had been the whole idea behind the trip in the first place (and the reason I didn't call back to the safe, sterile suburbs for help). A boy longs to get away from home, and how much farther away can he get than homelessness? Even though I was grubby and miserable, I was proud of my resource-fulness and my stick-to-itiveness, and pleased to see the bland boy drowning in my wake.

I peeled back the gauze on my arm and stared at the coag-ulating hole.

"I oughta do that sometime," Jules said.

"I don't know why, man," I said, lighting a Kent. " You know, a lot of people faint."

He considered this while the massive profile of a tugboat glided by a few feet away on the Mississippi. "Hey, do you need anything?" he asked.

Though I never took a handout from him, Jules often bought me cigarettes, or wine, or a sandwich. He was simply kind, not like some of the other generous types, who only wanted to get me in their hotel rooms.

"No," I said. "I still got the eight bucks. I'm OK, man."

"How about if we go out to dinner?" he said.

I eagerly agreed.

"Where you wanna go?"

The Italian restaurant on Royal Street, I told him without hesitation. I had passed it many times on my nighttime walks while trying to keep warm.

He blinked a few times and scratched the back of his English grocer's head. "Tomorrow OK?" he said. "I have to give my aunt a bath tonight."

"Fine," I said.

"Six thirty?"

"I'll be there."

"Good," he said. "I have to go." And he rose and made his

way out of the square, hands in pockets, a few vagrants hitting him up one last time as he strolled away.

Well, now things were looking up. But if I was going out to dinner at a fancy restaurant, I needed a shower and a decent night's sleep for a change. And the only way to get either of those in my circumstances was to stay at the Baptist mission. So I bought a sandwich (at a restaurant where I could pee), a quart bottle of Concord-grape wine (for the rejuvenation of my blood cells, you understand), and a pack of cigarettes (my only real friends), and strolled down to the library to kill the rest of the afternoon. At sunset I got in line for a bed at the mission. Every night, especially during Mardi Gras season, the mission filled quickly, and if you didn't get there early you'd be shut out.

I paid the $3.25 admission and trudged alongside the sour-smelling old men up the stairs to a room with a hundred bunk beds. I found a bed along the wall and hung my clothes over the rail. An old man approached me, his face like a withered croco-dile's. "Could you take the top one?" he said.

"I don't mind," I said, and climbed aloft.

The mattress was as thin as an X-ray of a broken back. The beds all creaked, and the men whistled and barked their stringy TB phlegm until it sounded like a factory where harbor seals made wooden clocks. The pillow was a flat mat of straw. The sheets felt sandy and slick, as if they hadn't been washed for months. I teetered up there like a mountain goat in the dark-ness, with my small thoughts, feeling dizzy, as if I might topple. The moon was stuck in one tall, arched window. Then, without warning, the lights went off. I listened to the ancient ones gurgle and saw. The young ones were out cavorting, and here I was in bed at 8 p.m., tired, grimy, half drunk, and feeling as old and washed up as my bunkmate. I will never sleep through all this racket and this stench of unwashed flesh, I thought.

Eventually I drifted off and dreamt I was Irish but no one could understand me. Then the lights were on again. It was still dark outside and the room was cold and hung with the sour miasma of cheap wine distilled through sweat glands. There must have been some mistake. "What time is checkout?" I mumbled. The missionaries or ministers or whatever they were had all assembled like drill instructors, hands on hips, their bullhorn voices urging us up and at 'em. If they woke us up at 4 a.m., the wisdom went, we could get a jump on finding work. Bones creaked and farts cracked. We lowered our heads and trudged naked in a mandatory car-wash line through the showers. I scrubbed and scrubbed and watched the tarlike dirt spinning across the tiles and down the drain. Shivering under a few swipes of a damp towel, I put my dirty clothes back on. Breakfast was a metal plate full of grits and burnt gravy. "You gonna finish yours?" asked the man with the crocodile face.

Manpower was just down the street. It paid a buck an hour for the crappiest jobs you can think of: scraping barnacles, scooping cemetery muck, sandblasting. I didn't want to work, but the blood money—one meal, one pack of smokes, one bottle of wine, one bed, and one shower—was gone, and I didn't want to be broke at the restaurant tonight, even if Jules was buying. So I got in line. The man in front of me suddenly broke rank, strolled to the curb, opened his jaws, and launched a gusher of what appeared to be liquid moonlight. He returned to his place in line as if nothing had happened. His buddy then promptly walked to the curb and vomited too. Wiping his mouth with the back of his hand, he said matter-of-factly: "It always makes me puke when I see someone else puke."

"My sister is the same way," said the first guy.

The line began to move, and I entered a lobby full of wrecked and rumpled-looking men, some of whom I recognized from the mission. When it was my turn to talk to the man at the desk, he drew a card from a file. "You know where Skaggs is?" he said.

I didn't even know what it was. It sounded like a brothel of ancient prostitutes or a clinic for rare skin disorders.

"It's a department store," he explained, opening a street map. "'Bout three miles. You can catch the bus here—transfer here." He stabbed the map with an index finger. "Can you be there by seven?"

The clock on the wall said six. I had a quarter, but that was for food. I would have to walk. "Yeah, I can do it."

He handed over the card. I filled it out. "No address," I said.

He nodded. "Be there by seven," he repeated. "And you report back here with the card at the end of the day—we'll pay you then, right?"

The sun was just up, no evidence yet of its heat. All the elastic had gone out of my socks, and they slumped in a pile down into my stupid jungle boots. I stopped to pull them up and promised myself that today I would buy new ones. They were so old and dirty they felt like wool.

Right, left, right. Away from the old-world pageantry of the French Quarter and the seediness of the American side, New Orleans became a city like any other, full of drab secretaries and barking dogs and big Chevrolets in need of paint. I stopped at a convenience store and deliberated between a package of peanuts, a package of miniature powdered donuts, and a can of sardines. I leaned toward the sardines because the bones, skin, and oil would keep me going longer, but how would I eat them without a can opener, and what would the Skaggy people think if I showed up smelling of sour old men and dead fish? So I bought two bags of peanuts, two cents change. The sun was climbing, warming to its task. It was cold at night in New Orleans in March, but the days often got hot. I ate one package of peanuts on the fly, chewing them too fast. I ate the second bag more slowly.

When I got to the department store, I went inside to ask for instructions, but no one knew where I was supposed to go, so I was five minutes late by the time I arrived at the warehouse. The warehouse men laughed at me, but they were happy to see me, because they planned to kill me. A truck loaded with forty-pound bags of Friskies dog food was backed up against the dock. "Get on in there," said one of the men, "and start unloading."

Briefest job training I've ever had. I hopped up into the

truck and began to throw down the bags while the men below stacked them on pallets and drove away on forklifts. I did some quick arithmetic: ten thousand bags of dog food plus one skinny boy to unload them equaled me dead on the dusty floor in two hours. The trailer was stuffy with the warm odor of slaughtered horses and pulverized corn. My boys down below laughed and grinned at me. I'll show them, I thought, and I began to toss down the bags. The game to end my life had begun.

Half an hour later I was already flagging. Then one of my boys jumped into the truck, I thought to help, but it was only to set up a conveyor belt. The bags were stacked to the roof and I had to stand on my toes to drag the top ones down. I tried to concentrate on the Italian restaurant, the flecks of basil in the tomato sauce and the way warm mozzarella stretches from your teeth. The trailer was only forty feet long but it seemed deeper than the Holland Tunnel. The bags were endless. Soon my thin arms began to stiffen and cramp. I began to totter. My peanuts, grits, and gravy had burned up long ago. I huffed and heaved and tried to think of girls I wanted to screw. I pretended that if I couldn't finish the job I would be executed by a cruel queen who would eat my testicles with tartar sauce.

At last the trailer was empty. I was covered with sweat and dog-food dust, and my arms and the backs of my legs burned like wires, but I'd shown those grinning bastards. I was no common street crumb or weakling sap of a suburbanite.

"Come on out of there," ordered one of my stocky coworkers, still grinning at me. Now, I thought, climbing down, we'll sit in the shade of the warehouse and drink lemonade for a spell.

Instead someone had backed another trailer full of Friskies against the dock.

"How many more of them are there?" I said, trying not to sound too helpless.

"Many as you want," he said

For lunch I lay on a four-wheel cart, smoked two Kent cigarettes, and stared at the sky.

It got hot in the afternoon, with the sun beating against the south wall of the trailer. I had lost a few pounds and had to tie my pants up with a piece of string. My muscles were finished, cooked, kaput. I dropped a bag, and it split and spilled. My boys laughed. I dropped another bag. "Hey, take it easy man." "Let him take a break." "He OK. You OK?" They grinned at each other.

After I fell down and cut my elbow, one of the men jumped in and helped. He worked double time, and I struggled along in feeble imitation, lifting bags that felt as if they were filled with rocks. The others had stopped grinning, however. I had finally won their respect. They respected me so much, they let me sweep the warehouse floor after we were through.

It was near sundown when I hobbled away from Skaggs, half deaf and doing the Frankenstein march with one knee not cooperating, the traffic like tweedy jazz in my ear. The clouds were a numb Halloween color. Power lines crackled above, just like the fizzle of my frayed nerves. My boots flopped around on the ends of my ankles. The thought of the Italian restaurant was all that kept me from falling over sideways into the gutter. And I had worked two hours overtime—ten hours total. That had to be at least thirteen bucks. If I played it right [bugle fanfare here], two days off.

But when I finally got back to Manpower and gave the man my voucher, he reached into the drawer and brought out a ten-dollar bill, snapping it somehow with a finger as he laid it in my palm. "Here you go, son."

I stared at it.

"Anything wrong?"

"I worked ten hours."

"That's what you get for ten hours. This is an employment service."

"No overtime?"

"You got overtime."

Yeah, right, all right. But it was 6:00 p.m., and let's not quibble over pennies. There was a team of expert Italian cooks poised for my arrival, and I would not keep them waiting. I was used to hot dog sandwiches from the mission, carroty gruel from the soup lines, an occasional po' boy or oyster muffuletta when I had the money. And I was old enough, eighteen, to drink wine in New Orleans. I hoped my legs would hold out.

And I wasn't going to work tomorrow. I was going to sleep all day in the grass in the sun at Jackson Square, then buy myself a bottle of fortified wine. The only thing that could ruin this Elysian vision was rain. It rained in Hawaiian proportions in New Orleans. I had never lived in a place where it rained so much. But it doesn't look like rain, I thought, as a raindrop splashed off the tip of my nose. Another splat against the back of my hand. I looked up.

I estimated a mile to Royal Street when the clouds just let go. It was that famous green New Orleans rain, like someone turning a lake upside down on your head. I dashed across the street and took cover in the doorway of a shoe-repair shop. The rain came with a vengeance, dark Gulf rain with shots of silver in it. The gutters swelled. The street shone like a river stippled by sweeping drifts of falling water. I lit a Kent and watched the silver green downpour switch back and forth in the streetlights and wondered how long Jules would wait for me. I kept pressing my face against the window of the shoe-repair shop to check the clock on the wall. Finally, my margin of error whittled to seconds, I stepped out into the torrent, head tilted forward, clinging as close as I could to the overhangs and awnings, and doggedly made my way.

Slogging through the deluge, my supposedly waterproof army-surplus jacket leaked like a fishnet. My jungle boots were designed to let out moisture, not keep out moisture, so the water flowed right through them. I felt my blue jeans picking up weight as they became saturated. My socks were bunched now in wads under my feet.

At last I came to the Italian restaurant. The rain beat a dull spongy drumbeat on my wool-capped head and raced in icy rivulets down my neck and back. Through the rain-streaming glass I saw Jules sitting by himself at a table in the middle of the busy dining room. I stood under the awning for a minute or two and tried to stomp off some of the water. I took off my wool cap and wrung it out like a dishrag.

As I stepped up into the restaurant and the door clattered shut behind me, every head turned on its neck like Japanese periscopes trained on the USS *Missouri*. The waiters stopped in their tracks, trays suspended, and I felt suddenly like a woman in a leotard on a spinning wooden wheel in front of expert knife throwers on *The Ed Sullivan Show*. I hovered in the entryway, shivering and dripping. I might have been the aquatic creature just emerged from the Black Lagoon. The captain behind the podium, with his twiggy French mustache, stared at me in disbelief. He would've normally asked me to leave, I'm certain, had I not hastily told him I had a reservation, with Jules right over there, for 6:30 p.m. And perhaps, because of my jungle boots and camouflage jacket—it wouldn't have been the first time—he mistook me for a GI.

I sounded like a trained porpoise slopping and squeaking my way across the room on the heels of the twiggy French mustache. This was a much fancier restaurant than my peeks in the window had indicated. The ceilings were high with spinning fans, and everything in the room was white: the drapes, the linen napkins, the tablecloths, the heat of my embarrassment. With every step, more water squeezed from my socks and flowed out the side vents of my boots. "Hello, Jules," I said, peeling off my dripping jacket and draping it over the back of my chair. I would not have been surprised to see goldfish jump out of the pockets.

The captain made a show of setting down the menu in front of me. Jules swallowed and offered a labored smile. He wore a snazzy white sweater with Navajo geometry across the breast. His hair was more carefully combed than usual, glistening from rain or pomade. My teeth began to chatter. I took off my hat, stuffed it in my jacket pocket, and mopped my face with a napkin.

"Glad you could make it," Jules said, giving it his best.

"Hit a bit of a storm on the way," I explained, grinning like that guy in the plasma joint before he'd hit the tiles.

"I bet you're hungry," he said.

"Yes," I said. "I've been thinking about this all day. It got me through eight trailers of dog food."

He tried another smile. For all the attention we received, we might've been newlywed transvestites, or a pair of flamenco dancers with maracas in our hands. The vicious whispering all around made my teeth chatter harder. Out the corner of my eye I saw a gray puddle creeping slowly from under our table and out across the white linoleum floor. I'd never been in a place more brightly lit than this. Why couldn't I have chosen a dark restaurant? Why did we have to sit in the very center of the dining room?

"What are you going to have?" said Jules.

I glanced at the menu and set it down. "I'll have the spaghetti with sausages," I said.

"That sounds good," said Jules, setting his menu on top of mine. "With garlic bread. Yes? And we'll have some wine, too."

God bless you, I thought.

While the waiter ignored Jules's attempts to catch his eye, I told Jules about my day at Skaggs, speaking in a loud voice so that these good people in their dry clothes with their wallets full of money would understand that I was not some verminous scamp or flower child heavily influenced by J. R. R. Tolkien, but a character out of a John Steinbeck novel, a truthful man of the road who earned his own way, just as Jules imagined me. It hadn't been my plan to become a tramp, and neither was it my intention to remain one.

At last the waiter deigned to visit our table. He held his chin so high I feared his head would tear loose and float away. Jules ordered for both of us while I clasped my hands between my knees and watched the terrible gray puddle crawl out across the tiles.

The wine came in a carafe. I poured some into my water

glass and dashed off three gulps, easing both thirst and humiliation. Jules watched me with a combination of admiration and pity in his English grocer's eyes. The kitchen doors swung open and closed, and the waiters transporting their whirling delicacies moved around us in frigid planetary arcs. The gray puddle continued to advance. I squeezed my toes down into my filthy wet socks and finished my wine. I wanted to get up and use the bathroom because there were no public restrooms, not one, in the French Quarter, and the business owners made it so difficult for anyone besides paying customers to use their facilities that I had peed my pants twice before discovering parks and alleys. But I didn't dare stand—they would've booted me for sure— so I poured another glass of the Italian red and tried to think of something to say.

When the spaghetti came, it looked like a four-foot-high beehive with whole, glistening sausages sticking out the sides. Overwhelmed with a Christmas-like euphoria, I attacked the twirled red noodles with my fork. The spaghetti was so good I almost cried. I ate like a grateful dog. The rain pattered against the glass. Jules tried to order another carafe of wine. I wanted to hold up my glass to the cooks for a toast, but the busboy came out with a mop and began to slap at the spreading gray puddle. Then one of the cooks, a puffy-eyed grouch with speckles on his face, like the skin of an overripe banana, came out to mop along the other side.

I tried to ignore the moppers. I wanted to enjoy the dry warmth, the wine, the food, and the gentle company of Jules. I took out a cigarette, but it was too wet to light, so I dropped it on the table. The cook mopped with short angry strokes and an occasional glance of loathing at me. Finally I got up and took the mop from the busboy's hands. He let it go, shrinking away so that he wouldn't accidentally touch me. I began to mop. The cook's mop and mine collided, and he glared at me. I had never felt so hated. I wrung the mop and slapped it back into the puddle. The cook leaned on his handle and glared while I made a few more passes, wrung the mop, and left it standing in the wringer. The cook snorted with disgust. I wished I was a Golden Gloves boxer. I considered throwing my ten bucks on the table. I thought once more of using the restroom. Instead I left the restaurant.

Jules was waiting for me outside, wearing a look like a mother whose boy has gone to jail.

"Sorry about all that, Jules," I said.

"You couldn't help it," he said. "You can't help it if it rains."

The cook stuck his head out the door. "Don't be loitering around out here now," he said with a scowl. "Management don't want no bums hanging around the door."

I thought Jules might offer something in our defense. This was his city, after all. He belonged to its middle class and shopped in its well-lighted grocery stores. But he only looked away.

"We're paying customers," I said.

"Get along now," said the cook, flicking his fingers at me. "Before I have to come out there and move you."

Another Golden Gloves moment passed, and Jules and I shuffled along to the next awning, which dripped steadily like a cage made of blue rain. We lingered for a minute, nothing to say. I wondered where I would sleep, how I would stay warm, how I would dry my clothes, how I would make ten bucks last three days. I wondered how I would ever save enough money to go north.

"I gotta go," said Jules. "I'll see you at the square." He almost shook my hand. I could see he wanted to do something more: give me money, invite me to sleep on his couch while he drank hot chicory with cream and read to his crippled aunt from *The Wind in the Willows*. But instead he walked off into the rain.

I haven't thought of Jules much since. Once I got out of New Orleans, I never returned, except passing through a few times on my way to somewhere else. Whenever I look back on that reckless time, I think of being dirty, hungry, and cold. I think of walking through a cold night and wondering if the sun would ever come. I think of eating a piece of abandoned birthday cake

on a park bench and considering the invitation of a man I didn't
know to come up to his hotel room. I think of the Mississippi slug-
ging along, too big for itself, swirling against the rocks, the
water so high the ships and barges seemed to slide by above me.
I knew nothing then and neither did I care about the fragile
levees or Lake Pontchartrain (except it had the word "rain" in it).
I was barely aware that most of the city was below sea level.

When the hurricanes came, first Katrina, and three weeks
later Rita, to destroy the city of New Orleans—dropping rain in
a volume far beyond anything I had ever known—I began to think
of Jules again. If he's still alive, he's around fifty, my age, and
I imagine that his aunt is dead, and that he has continued to
romanticize the homeless and sponsor them in his peculiar way.
Whether he evacuated or had flood insurance or surrendered to
fate likely made little difference as his city went under. His home
was gone—toilet, hot water, clean socks, electricity, a ham sandwich with mayonnaise and sweet pickles—and it was his turn
finally to live the adventure, a world of trouble worse than mine.

My Pink Tombstone

for Julie Carpenter

IN SPRING OF 1988 I BECAME THE CARETAKER OF A twenty-acre plot my sister and her husband had bought as a prospective retirement location in the Black Forest of Colorado: elevation 8,200 feet. It was a great opportunity for me to write and reflect and rest up from the roaring hellfire on earth. The rent was free, and I got a little caretaking stipend because my sister and her husband were generous and understood that I wasn't doing well financially. My responsibilities were minimal: I had to make sure the worms didn't eat the trees, the roof of the old single-wide trailer didn't leak, the pipes didn't freeze, potential vandals didn't wander onto the property, and developers from California didn't come along and try to put up chain motels and plastic hamburger stands.

The locale was lonely and isolated, so my sister gave me a golden retriever puppy to keep me company. I had been unhappy for a while and had recently thought of killing myself, but the dog changed all that: at first because she took up so much of my time, crapping and peeing all over the carpet in our little trailer and running off into the dark and towering woods; and later because I grew attached to her. I'd never been able to have a dog before, because I moved around a lot, and you can't take a dog on a bus or keep pets in a rooming house or a residential motel.

My golden retriever was smaller than most, so I named her Shorty. She had a glossy reddish coat, a sweet disposition, and no ability at all to retrieve. Once, she ran after a stick I threw into the middle of a lake, and she almost drowned. Another time we got lost in the woods, and she was no help at all finding the way back home. I had a hunting dog that didn't retrieve, couldn't swim, and had no sense of direction. We were together constantly. I took her for two walks a day, three if you count the mile-long stroll down to the mailbox. I taught her to sit, stay, lie down, and come in response to hand signals. I slept on the floor of the trailer, because my back gave me trouble and the bedroom was cold and haunted, and Shorty slept in the crook of my legs. She was keen on spaghetti, corn cakes, and popcorn. She loved snow. When it got down to thirty below and I was blowtorching the pipes under the trailer to thaw them, she trotted around outside as if it were noon of a summer's day. She was so eager to please that if I gave her a lamb chop she wouldn't eat it until I told her it was all right. I'd always thought it pitiful how dog owners gushed about their pets and blubbered when they died, but now I understood.

Being caretaker in the Black Forest was as close as I had come to Paradise on earth, but after ten months my sister and her husband decided to sell the property. They wouldn't be retiring for at least thirty years, and Colorado real estate was in a tailspin. Paradise went poof, just like in the books. But now that I had old Shorty, my elegant and noble companion, I felt I could face anything. I loaded up my sister's Mazda pickup with my few belongings, told my confused dog to hop on in, and we jostled down the long dirt drive and out of the Black Forest.

It was late March, and there was still snow on the ground in the foothills. I wasn't sure where to go. Everyone else was migrating west or south, so it felt right to go north and east. Except for the year and a half I'd lived in Niagara Falls, I'd spent little time in that part of the country.

The cities and freeways confused Shorty. At the motel where we spent the first night she ran from the room and tried to get back in the truck. After a while, though, she got into the rhythm of traveling, and I believe she enjoyed the new places and scenery and smells. We stopped often to look over small towns that might have been good places to live. We had long talks, the lonely man and his dog. We stayed in motels and watched movies and ballgames and read the local papers. I couldn't bring her into a restaurant or a grocery store, and I didn't want to leave her alone in the car, so when it was time to eat we often went to the drive-through at McDonald's. Every time old Shorts saw the golden arches she began to pad her feet on the seat. She always ate her sandwiches the same way: bread first, then cheese, then meat. Outside of the ticks she picked up in Bardstown, Kentucky, which I squeezed as they rose like drops of blood from her coat, the only bad part of the trip was the vague fear that we would soon be separated.

On a whim I veered north and went to Niagara Falls to see some old friends, an old girlfriend in particular. I stayed with my former boss at the bar where I'd been a famous alcoholic bartender, but it snowed the whole time, and I got depressed because the old girlfriend was living with the guy she'd left me for. Money running out, I wrote a note ("It's snowin' so I'm blowin'") and headed down to Chestertown, Maryland, to visit my old best friend Stiff Cliff, who was losing his mind from booze, and his wife, Denise the Christian shrew, who, apparently unable to contain the charity and grace of her faith, screamed at me whenever she got the chance. Later, powerless to resist that gushing conduit of love from God, she accused me of making a pass at her in the kitchen, and Stiff Cliff believed her. He and I haven't spoken civilly since. I suppose we were never really friends if he couldn't trust me. He also had an electric fence surrounding his house. Shorty got shocked a couple of times, and Stiff Cliff thought it was funny.

Before I managed to escape, the Christian shrew lined me up a job with a friend of hers, a ship captain in Camden, Maine. He was renovating a turn-of-the-century schooner and hoped to find a cook; I had cooked in a dozen or so kitchens. It looked to me like Paradise again (careful, careful), sailing around the islands of Penobscot Bay, whipping up fine cuisine in the galley, standing shirtless on the prow in my sailor pants with the wind parting my hair, scrambling up to the crow's nest from time to time to shout, "Land ho!"

I couldn't bring Shorty with me on a boat, so I decided to leave her with my sister. I'd only be gone for a few months, I explained to Shorty, and since I'd be at sea the whole time and unable to spend money, I would have saved enough cash by the fall for us to move back to the mountains or the forest. You'll see, I told her. Temporary separation wouldn't be so bad. She didn't seem to trust the idea, however, and stuck close to me the whole three-thousand-mile drive back to my sister's house in Southern California. I had to move fast if I wanted the job, so I dropped off the truck and the dog with my sister, then grabbed a flight to Boston, got airsick on a small commuter plane to Portland, Maine (and here I was going to work on a boat), and arrived in cold gray Camden by bus, flat broke.

The aged schooner was in a shambles under its rough tarp. It essentially needed to be rebuilt in a little more than two months, as it was already booked for several weeklong cruises in June. My employer, Captain Toil, was a likeable chap with thick glasses that distorted his eyes. I had no shipbuilding experience, so I was thrown into the general labor pool, which consisted mostly of kids who hoped to sail but had little chance of being selected. There would be only six crew members: Captain Toil, the first mate (a professional sailor, already hired), the cook (me, hopefully), the mess mate, and deckhands one and two.

We had our work cut out for us. Many of the old salts who came around predicted that we wouldn't make the deadline. Captain Toil drove his team hard, with mandatory twelve- and sixteen-hour days toward the end, and no days off. Though the schooner was named the Adventure, I came to think of her as the *Juggernaut,* for her power to crush every last soul unfortunate enough to enlist under her banner.

After a couple of weeks I was penciled in as the cook. I had proved myself worthy by sanding, painting, planing, and heaving about great timbers, some of which weighed four hundred pounds, and by being the only one of the many hopeful sailing candidates with any real cooking experience. I was eager to get into the galley. I've never been good with wood or tools, and, soft suburban lad that I am, I don't like breathing the fumes from a pot of paint thinner or feeling my right arm vibrate all night after ten hours operating an electric sander. But before I could start cooking, we had a boat to finish.

More and more men came to work as the deadline to sail approached. Originally there had been seven or eight of us laboring on scaffoldings, or astride the great planer, or across the planks of the ruined decks, and three of us sleeping in the boathouse above the mighty Juggernaut. But as summer pressed in I could no longer count the number of carpenters, ship-wrights, painters, and general laborers who'd become involved, twelve of whom eventually lived in the boathouse, packed in sleeping bags across the floor, waiting in line to use the one and only shower and the one and only microwave. I went to live in the tool trailer, where I could read by flashlight with no one's smelly feet in my face and not have to worry about that mad bas-tard of a shipwright who came in drunk at four in the morning and wanted "to fuck someone."

You may recall that Paradise is traditionally followed by the Fall. After many twelve-hour days lifting those four-hundred-pound timbers, working in cramped quarters, and inhaling dust and paint fumes, I developed a bad cough and began to lose weight. I can't count the number of times I cracked my head on the scaffolding and was literally knocked flat into the sawdust. But the thought of my reunion with Shorty sustained me. It would only be a few months. Time goes by fast. Why couldn't it go by faster?

The week before we were to set sail—only days after we'd heaved the Juggernaut into the bay to fit the masts—I began cook-ing in the galley, a sort of a dry run for some of the shipwrights and the crew. My handpicked messmate, Cal of Happy Endings, a steady young man with an Ivy League future who worshiped Hemingway, helped me sling out the meals and wash dishes in the tiny sink. The absence of electricity and other modern comforts supposedly enhanced the ship's rustic charm. Water was heated through pipes that circulated through the woodstove. Large blocks of ice would eventually be hoisted in through the hatches for refrigeration. The fire in the stove had to be maintained constantly to keep proper heat. To have breakfast cooked by eight o'clock, you needed a fire started by six. Cooking on board a ship was turning out to be a bigger challenge than I had thought.

By arrangement, a few passengers arrived a day early, and I baked a humpbacked birthday cake (oven too hot) for a man named George Ford. He and his traveling companions were understandably dismayed by the undeveloped state of the ship, the great commotion of the workers, and, no doubt, the shape of their cake. Captain Toil put them in the only cabins that had been completed. The next day, the rest of the passengers began to arrive, and supplies were laid in, along with the blocks of ice. Not all the cabins were finished, so the would-be passengers milled about on deck, toed the scuppers, and peeked over the side at the oil slicks while the carpenters sawed and banged away and the painters hurried to slap on paint.

My cabin was one of the ones not finished, and I had spent the previous few nights sleeping on a bench in the galley. After I cooked lunch for forty, the tourists, many of whom had booked this trip months in advance, began to filter down out of boredom to talk to me and acquaint themselves with my life story as I began preparations for dinner. They had many special requests, allergy specifications, dietary restrictions, and so on. Then like an inventor swept up by the sudden force of a revolutionary idea, I realized that I did not want to cook breakfast, lunch, dinner, and afternoon snack for twenty-nine people on an old leaky woodstove in a cramped galley with a bad cough and my pants falling off under the frosty brow of Captain Toil for the rest of the summer, so I hastily packed my bag, scuttled up from my hole, and made for the gunwales.

There was a burst of applause as I jumped down onto the dock below. I did not look back to see who was clapping, though I suspect it was unanimous: frustrated shipwrights, painters, and last-minute carpenters, and especially those who had paid to be out on the open water by now with the sun on their noses and the sea breeze in their hair and someone baking cupcakes for them in the galley below. I still don't know if the *Juggernaut* ever sailed.

As I walked away whistling, I had in my possession one hastily packed bag and four hundred dollars in cash. (I resigned the notion of ever collecting all the wages owed to me.) I found the bus station closed, but it was a warm late afternoon and I had nothing pressing to do, and no idea where I was going anyway. There was only the eventual goal of making enough money to retrieve Shorty and settle down in a cabin in the woods.

I spent an hour in the sunny window of the dank but well-stocked library trying to read Proust, still too excited by my reckless departure to absorb much of what I read. The librarians seemed especially enticing this late afternoon, their bodies outlined in electricity, their buns verily tingling. I've always been drawn to librarians: these are the women who take care of the books. But I had become afraid of women due to my inability to make sense of them and the strange way they often looked at me when I was completely in earnest. The library was closing soon, so I sauntered back downtown and sat on the bench in front of the bus station. As the sun sank, I enjoyed that wonderful tranquility of leaving a terrible job, even if another one was waiting right around the corner.

To my surprise, along in their Subaru came my hand-picked messmate, Cal of Happy Endings, who had also jumped ship, and his friend Flamboyant Jerry, a thin-armed kid who had worked several weeks with us, renovating the ship and admiring the men as they came out of the shower. They had my French chef's knife and my alarm clock, which I had left in my haste, and they offered me a ride to Frederick, Maryland, where Flamboyant Jerry lived. He said I would like Frederick, claimed it was affordable, and since it sounded as good a place as any, I threw my bag into the back and climbed into the car.

We drove through the rain down the turnpikes, past the regimentally eerie Howard Johnson complexes, stopping for snacks and gas and trying not to feel lost or overwhelmed by these densely flowing Eastern Rivers of Humanity. We all felt shakily proud of our bold failure. We were beatnik symbols of giddy freedom. We were freed slaves. (The wage for working on the boat was to have been two dollars an hour, plus meals and accommodations; there was the joy of sailing, too, I suppose, but I have never enjoyed sailing that much.) I was the scatterbrained leader of the screwups. My brash act had liberated these kids and allowed them to return home with no money and treat it like a victory. Recognizing my influence over their impressionable, romantic minds, I discoursed freely upon various half-baked ideas such as Christ as Abraham Lincoln, the importance of getting your nose broken in a swimming pool, determination versus Free Willie, and the color at the top of the rainbow made from human sadness that all the gods clamor to see.

At last we found a restaurant that wasn't a Howard Johnson's. Our waitress had a speech impediment, and when she inquired about dessert, Flamboyant Jerry insisted she recite the names of the pies over again, hoping to hear her say, "Gwam-quackah-cwust," just once more. She slapped down the check and stalked away while Jerry cried with laughter. He had a cruel streak despite his love of men and sailing. He also had some sort of peculiar candy allergy and could only eat Zagnut Bars. Thus all down the eastern seaboard commenced the Great Hunt for the Zagnut Bar. It was a creditable diversion, akin to that license plate game children often play on cross-country car trips, although we had no luck finding Zagnuts.

That night we stayed with friends of Jerry's in Waynesboro, Pennsylvania, a pleasantly drowsy town with newspapers yellowing in the racks and old men covered with cobwebs on park benches. I would've liked to have rented an apartment there and sent for Shorty, but there was nothing—not an outhouse, tree house, lighthouse, or charnel house—for less than four hundred a month. Jerry's friends were out, so we never met them, only saw their fish tank full of gerbils and dozens of boxes of breakfast cereal arranged like books on top of the refrigerator. The apartment was as hot as a reptile cage, and I slept poorly on the couch. And there were no Zagnuts to be found in Waynesboro, either.

The novelty of quitting a job wears off about as quickly as a six-pack of beer, and by the time we'd reached Frederick, we were just three sober young men out of work. Frederick was an agreeable town, however, with Zagnuts in abundance. We found our first Zagnut Bars at a liquor store downtown (they are white candy bars, generally uninspiring, made at that time by the same company that produced the Clark Bar), and I ate two. Flamboyant Jerry invited me to stay at his apartment, where we were greeted by a man in a kimono, who turned out to be Jerry's roommate. I picked up a newspaper to check the rents and saw that Frederick was no cheaper than Pennsylvania or any other place I'd investigated in the last several months. I was growing discouraged about my future. I hardly had enough money to be a decent homeless person in the East.

A party formed that night—Jerry had many friends—and I felt suddenly old and tired and out of place. Uncomfortable even at the smile of a pretty young girl, I feigned exhaustion and went to bed early. The next morning I got up with the sun and, without so much as a thank-you, slipped out and trudged across town to search for the bus depot. Not knowing where it was, I looked for poor neighborhoods, greeting many winos, and making many wrong turns. I even broke down and asked directions, but to no avail. Finally, in an impotent rage, I smashed my bag against a pole, breaking my alarm clock and powdering a bunch of aspirins. A minute later the bus depot magically appeared (prayer and sacrifice do work!), and I bought a one-way ticket for Hot Springs, Arkansas, because I had finally given up hope of ever living in the East. I had been warned many times against living in the South, home of rednecks, lynch mobs, and cross-eyed inbred banjo players with bad teeth, but all this suddenly seemed interesting to me and pointed auspiciously to the possibility of affordable rent and getting back my dog.

The Hot Springs bus depot was across the street from a boarded-up hotel. Except for the fairly new depot, the whole area was lush with weeds and seemed abandoned. I walked aimlessly for a long while, trying to get the odd lay of this gambling resort along the boundary of a national park. Hotels and room rentals seemed abundant, but all were wrong for one reason or another. After many miles I finally came upon the Best Motel: eighty-five a week, ceiling fan, kitchenette, and dark curtains to my liking. Neither the TV nor the oven worked, but it had a deep, tiled shower, and the mattress was firm.

I stayed at the Best Motel, slept, drank red wine, shook the aspirin dust from my clothes, and looked for a job. Hot Springs had the right feel. It was a bit hot for Shorty, but I still thought she'd like it. The rent was cheap (you can almost always tell by the motel rates), and the people were at least outwardly friendly. There were lots of tire places and catfish huts and newly opened nightclubs, and plenty of jobs at very low pay. I applied at several restaurants, two nightclubs, a hospital, and the Holiday Inn.

At last I got an interview at the prestigious Arlington Hotel, which stood thirty feet above street level, like an island at the head of Bathhouse Row, a strip of mostly closed but regal old bathhouses. Across from the Row was an eruption of campy tourist attractions—Coney Island grafted onto downtown Tijuana—with such memorable exhibitions as the counting chicken and a Madame Tussaud's Wax Museum.

At the Arlington I checked in at personnel and then climbed a long, steep flight of stairs to a door marked *Employees*

Only Beyond This Point—as if anyone else would undertake this Mayan escalade. Opening the door, I entered a massive ball-room of a kitchen, alive with clanging pots, roaring flames, and hissing jets of steam. I moved carefully along the slick ceramic tiles while everyone eyed me from their work stations as if I were an evil invader from the planet Herpes.

The chef was about thirty-two, with straight black hair that he kept whipping back out of his eyes. He wore tall black clogs that looked slippery. Apparently satisfied with my work history, he sat across the desk from me, fingertips together, and said with a straight face, "You don't use dope, do you?"

I replied with an equally straight face that I didn't.

"I can't get good help because no one can pass the drug test," he said, gesturing futility.

And isn't it funny that I hadn't smoked pot in four years, except nine days earlier with the shipwrights at a card game, just for the hell of it?

I had never thought of cooking as being important enough to warrant a drug test. What difference does it make if the french fries are a little darker today? But I drank a lot of water and crossed my fingers and peed in the cup and passed the test and won that minimum-wage job. Later I discovered that half the people who worked there used dope, including and espe-cially that straight-faced doper, the chef.

The Arlington had three bustling restaurants. Because of my cooking experience (I neglected to mention the four days in a ship's galley on a woodstove) I was assigned to the Fountain Room, "the finest gourmet restaurant in Arkansas," according to our accident-prone, constantly-slipping-on-his-clogs, dope-smoking chef, who could usually be found in the poolroom across town. The Fountain Room served mostly nouvelle cuisine, which is small portions of quail and veal kidney and the like on hot plates with a muck of fancy sauces and tricky garnishes such as cucumbers fanned into birds of paradise and radishes carved into Mount Rushmore and all sorts of other needless fooling around to entertain the rich, who need more noodles in their diet, in my opinion.

I was not immediately embraced by the people of Hot Springs. Rarely, to be fair, am I immediately embraced anywhere, but I had this expectation that the South would be more hospitable than the rest of the country. It wasn't. A mentally handicapped dishwasher actually called me a Yankee on my second day, and I felt as if I'd done something wrong, until I remembered that the North was the side that opposed slavery.

When I got my first paycheck I was literally down to a nickel, but soon I was making seven hundred a month, and since you can't have a dog in a motel, I checked out an apartment for rent down the way that allowed pets. As the landlady led me up the stairs she stopped, her false teeth flopping around in her jaws like a mouse with its tail caught in a trap, and confided to me: "We don't rent to colored here. It isn't that we're prejudiced. It's just that colored and white don't get along."

The apartment was furnished: two big chairs, a bathtub, a table, and a bed. My neighbors were indeed all white—or at least, they looked white, the notion of pure race being a fallacy in America—and half of them were crazy, like Jake, an old, muttering, droopy-drawered cracker who'd stroll uninvited into my kitchen and start looking over my personal items as if he had stumbled upon a yard sale; and Vida, who smoked so much I believe it was she who eventually burned the place down.

Summer, which lasts six or seven months in that part of the world, was well underway: the shrill *chee-chee-chee* of the parakeets and the apes swinging past the windows on vines and the mosquitoes feeding lustily and the magnolia and the morning glory and the golden jonquil all laden with heavy, twinkling drops from the thunderstorms that passed over without fail every forty-two minutes. The heat in my un-air-conditioned second-floor apartment was a killer. The brick walls would bake all day in the sun, and at night, when I got home from work and sat in my big green armchair, I felt like a roasting chicken without the benefit of salt and pepper. It was so hot my thumbs would sweat. The bathtub was hot to the touch. I wanted to send for Shorty, but it wouldn't have been kind to leave her in this brick kiln all day while I was gone. She seemed happy with my sister, and I thought it better to keep saving money, find a more agreeable situation, and pick her up the following spring.

While I waited for my savings to accumulate and Southern hospitality to kick in, a recently hired Mexican waitress named Claudia, who spoke terrible English, began to flirt with me near the steam table. She was svelte, in her twenties, with mildly aquiline features—French blood, I imagined, mingled with mestizo. I spoke barely functional kitchen Spanish. She offered me a ride home one day—my first. (You can't get much more southern or hospitable than Mexico.)

From the beginning, little alarms would go off in my head when Claudia came around. She was aggressive, prideful, and secretive. She drove a Chrysler Cordoba the color of a Martian dust storm. Her English was about as good as my Spanish, although she had no qualms telling me how bad my Spanish was. Because I wore a silly seventies porno mustache and one of those cotton Chef Boyardee hats at work, she insisted that I looked "Italiano."

Every time we worked together, she offered me a ride home, and living nearly three miles away, I always accepted. Once, we went to a bar, where she dragged me by the hand across the room to show me where she had removed pictures of herself from a bulletin board. The rest of the evening was taken up with her explanations of her high moral standards, which were somehow related to the removal of the photos. Her reluctance to discuss her past should have been a red flag, but Hot Springs is a gambling resort through which players, tourists, itinerants, and migrants constantly flowed. Nor was I nosy about possible immigration issues. And though she intimated that she had several children by several different fathers, she never seemed in any hurry to get home to feed anyone or hang art projects on her refrigerator.

Eventually she came up to see my room. I knew from her lectures that she was not interested in sex, at least not outside of marriage, and especially not with a guy she barely knew. So we had a drink, and she studied my bare walls and talked about Mexico and the people at work. When it was time for her to go, she grew angry with me because I did not kiss her good night. Having totally missed the point, as usual, I kissed her, and then all at once the passion rose, the red rose, the silver thorn, the bloody rose.

It had been a long time since I'd had sex: years. Johnny Appleseed I wasn't. I had gotten out of the habit. I preferred the freedom of being unattached, of not having to grapple and lie. I preferred the purity of solitude and the raindrops pattering the drum skins of my window screens and sliding like glass beads down the necklaces of the telephone wires. I preferred sitting in my big green chair reading a book while my thumbs sweated. I preferred the simplicity of no emotional debt and getting on the bus when it was time to go without someone throwing vegetables at my window. Yet there was a stronger part of me—my reproductive system, I suppose—that cast the final vote that night.

The garments of the cook and the waitress fell to the floor. We wrestled and groaned. I felt like a big slobbery dog that had been drugged. Somewhere deep within me the tadpole spark caught, normalcy flourished, and we fell together into my hot bed under the spinning ceiling fan with the insects cheering outside.

"Fantastico!" she cried, sucking on my neck.

You're lying, I thought. But even though my purity and freedom were toppled like a pyramid of beer cans in a college dorm room, I felt good. I felt like a man. I felt alive. Yes, she was a bit unusual. Yes, there were a few husbands, or boyfriends, or biological fathers lurking in her past. Yes, she could now call me, drive under my window and honk her horn, demand to know my business, and slip into my room late at night while I was sleeping. But I had myself a girlfriend. Finally, I had myself a girl.

Except the next day when I came into work, she was gone. Not sick, not on vacation, not playing hooky, but gone. One of the dining-room captains said that she had tried earlier that morning to get her check but without success. She refused to leave an address for them to mail it to her. All I had to remember Claudia by was an earring she had dropped on my floor and a neckful of embarrassing hickeys.

We'd had unprotected sex, and I was immediately struck by two thoughts: 1) having children by different fathers is her hobby, and I may have sired a child I will never know; and 2) she hates men, or maybe just men who look Italian, and she gave me some viral parting gift.

A few weeks later I came down with yellow diarrhea and a debility like I had never known. I missed two days of work. A month later I was sick again, this time with flu symptoms. Sick again two weeks later, I knew the low-down and terrible truth: Claudia had given me AIDS.

Oh, how sad and foolish I had been to fall into such an obvious trap laid by a strange woman whose single purpose was to spread disease and suffering, to literally murder men. But sadder yet was a pink envelope I found in my mailbox one evening that October. Inside was a letter from my sister:

I have some very sad news. Shorty died last night. I don't know what she died from. She was healthy and happy and full of energy last time I saw her. I don't know if there was anything I could have done or not done. I don't know what else to tell you except I'm sorry. Paul is burying her between the fruit trees.

I cried then, letter in my lap, astounded by the depth of my attachment to this animal and the callousness with which I'd abandoned her for the pleasure of a sailing trip. I felt thrust back to the days when I was inconsolably alone and misunderstood. For the thousandth time I wondered at my ineptitude at forming relations with humans. Perhaps my peripatetic pattern was not a brave poetic sacrifice, "the life of the drifter," but rather a method by which I could indefinitely postpone the obligations of adulthood, love, and family. Pink letter in my lap splotched with tears, I vowed never to fail the test of loyalty again.

A few months later I moved to Vegas, where I could be invisible and make some money for a change. I got a job as a cook at the Hacienda, then at Binion's downtown. I got an HIV test, too, finally. Negative. Funny, it made little difference. When I wasn't cooking, I watched TV or worked at the little table in the kitchen on my Great Las Vegas Novel. And at night I kept having dreams about old Shorts: We were face to face in the grass, a knife between us. She was walking away from me on a beach. In the last dream she let me hold her. I took this for forgiveness.

Eighteen years later I still have the letter from my sister. My pink tombstone. My clean little knife. My neat, flat souvenir of betrayal.

Methamphetamine for Dummies

MY NEIGHBOR, A DIVORCED PSA MECHANIC WHO INVITES the children in and pours them draft beer to promote drug sales and his chances with the girls, offers me my first taste of methamphetamine at age fifteen. He calls it "crank," like the name of a car part or a grouchy old man. I've never snorted anything before. Crank looks nasty, like ant poison and pulverized glass, all chopped up on that mirror. Whiffing something straight up your nose into your brain seems a violation of human dignity, and tastes even worse, like the dirt from a vacuum cleaner bag. I try not to cry the burning pain is so terrible. I am certain I will sneeze blood all over the curtains. I think I've done permanent damage. But then comes the drip drip drip, that bitter alkaloid savor with which the meth user learns to associate pleasure, and I wander around grinding my jaws and feeling like Bruce Lee grafted onto Aldous Huxley for about twelve hours. It takes three days to weather the most desiccated and noxiously enervated hangover I've ever experienced. I vow never to do it again ("never again never again," the chant of the methhead), do it eight or nine more times, and then, as if God really loves me, crank vanishes from my neighborhood—and no one misses it.

Ten years later, dead broke, I come back to the old neighborhood to live with my parents for a few months, to write, as I explain it. I've quit school again. Seems that I'd learned one thing in college and that is that college is not for me. But I won't be here long. I just want to frame the novel about the redneck chiropractor with the crystal ball, hopefully sell it, make a little cash, and start the talk show and interview circuit. Even though I'm sufficiently talented, I suspect that I should've finished school, gotten a degree, weaved some sort of safety net, just in case the novel doesn't pan out, just in case I am a sham, but that seems gutless to me, even more gutless than coming back home to live with my parents.

This neighborhood hasn't changed much. Drawn out to thematic absurdity, these small drafty plywood ranch-style homes with their split-rail fences, wagon wheels, dangling branding irons, and varnished cow skulls remind me of the tacky little shacks on miniature golf courses. Thrown up in a big hurry back in 1957, many owners have not made much effort, despite rocketing California real estate prices, to keep their homes from becoming eyesores. I'm not surprised to see Meuenchau and Coombs just where I left them, sitting in Meuenchau's old pickup truck, smoking homegrown and listening to Leon Russell under the pepper tree. They wave at me, their eyes cheery slits. Howdy boys, I say. What's new? Not a whole lot, I see. How's the bass fishing? All right, just one toke, but then I gotta go . . .

My parents have always treated me kindly. My mother humors me because I'm her son. My father actually seems to understand. He would've been a writer too but he got seduced by alcohol and an early marriage and the need to bring home the bacon. Plus he is one of the few who knows that writing is pure torture and that to grab that diamond you must walk four thousand eighteen miles into hell. He'd rather watch the sprinklers and listen to the ballgame, a glass of German white wine in his hand. He's the only one, including me, who believes I will succeed.

But now at last a chance to write uninterrupted in a quiet house. Both my parents work so I have the whole morning and half the afternoon to myself. I spread all my junk out on the dining-room table, plenty of pens and paper. My eyes drift toward the newspaper. I doodle. I grow drowsy. Five more minutes pass. My muses must have gone to the moon. To keep from falling asleep I write a letter to a friend. Look at the prose explode! And there are so many books to read. I feel undereducated, probably because I keep quitting school, not to mention those wasted eons of whiskey drinkin' and tail chasin', so I drift to the couch and begin to undertake a book I admire or a neglected section of history or philosophy, and then maybe just a wee bit of a nap to let all the teeming thoughts and ideas soak in.

After a few months of sleeping in late, reading on the couch, and writing letters to friends, I decide I'd better get a job. I haven't sent out a single story, haven't finished one chapter in my redneck chiropractor novel. And I can't ask Dad for money anymore. Dad, can I have five dollars to go to the bar? And the way the neighbors look at me in this working-class neighborhood where I was once a gifted youth with a ticket out makes me feel like a snake in a toilet bowl. Anyway, labor is good for the soul. I have fashioned myself after that class of writer who is not afraid to get dirty, who can talk about an adze, a pallet jack, or a skip-loader without having to look them up in the dictionary.

Coombs and Meuenchau work in the barrio down on Logan Avenue not far from downtown San Diego in a chemical warehouse, where just about anyone can get a job, including me. Coombs and I are "parts pullers." We're handed a phoned-in requisition from a jobber, or parts retailer, and we fill a plastic crate with car wax, parts dip, Marvel Mystery Oil, fuel filters, brake fluid, engine starter, and the like, then pick up the next requisition. Meuenchau delivers these "parts" to the various retailers. The days go by fast enough, though by the time I get home the sun is almost gone and I'm too tired to write. Still, I don't feel ready to sit down to serious composition quite yet. Physical labor feels good. I feel "real" again. I don't have to ask Dad for money. The neighbors pound me fraternally on the back as I sit with them in their lawn chairs out in the driveway smelling the oil dripping from their Ford Rancheros and hoping their daughter comes out in her terry shorts as we lament (as every generation of humanity since the advent of language) the brevity of the days and the general decline of morality. And I'm writing all this down in my head, don't you fret: it's the Chemical Warehouse Novel, a real blue-collar gem.

Coombs, a runty blond with tossed rusty hair and a sharp Adam's apple, who I believe has some sort of undiagnosed form of Tourette's, but is too poor, simple, and uninterested to do anything about it (until the last twenty out of a million years in human history our flaws, quirks, idiosyncrasies, our "neurological disorders" were simply our "personalities"), grew up four houses down from me. I remember him in his baby carriage. I remember him catching me in the catwalk on the way to school one morning and going on and on about "the hound dog" until he showed me the Irish setter that had hung itself by jumping still hooked to its leash over a brick wall. Here he is ten years old drinking from a bottle of Ten High on the couch in a ramshackle gas-and-chicken-feather-smelling house piled high with furniture and trash, his mother in her muumuu glued to the telly. As I recall, he began smoking pot in the second grade. A high school dropout, Coombs is inclined to violence and can often be disruptive and obscene. He has a variety of tics. He claps, hops, and hoots. He screeches, coughs, barks, spits, grunts, gurgles, clacks, hisses, whistles, coyote whoops, gives you the finger, wants to arm wrestle (he's very strong), and finishes your sentence for you in a ghostly mumble that seems for a moment by his expression as if he is reading your mind. Marijuana ameliorates his symptoms, turns his jerking, aggression, and swearing into squirming, repetitive questions, giggly blank stares, and an occasionally pithy observation such as why do people have hair?

Meuenchau, twenty-nine, who lives on the next block over, is a slump-shouldered reed, his eyes Charlie Chan chinks in a Slavic face so thick it looks like a mask. His receding hair he wears in the Chinese detective mode, ponytail down the back. I would estimate his IQ at somewhere around seventy. Calm and steady as a tortoise, he hasn't had a girlfriend since he was eighteen.

He likes to sleep, smoke dope, and boat fish for bigmouth bass. Meuenchau lives with his mother (his father died of cancer a few years ago); he's never lived on his own.

After work I drink a beer or two, have dinner with my parents, watch or listen to the ballgame with my father, who has advanced himself to that insensate goal he manages to score most every night. I scribble a note or two (Ramon drove the fork-lift, blades raised, into the second deck, lifting up Fram County, it is high prairie now, foothills almost, and the wild sheep seem unsettled by the early snow). Then I am restless, loins astir, my warehouse muscles taut, my parched youth in need of a night's slaking. I walk past the suburban windows with the warm life inside and often end up on the next street over, where Meuenchau and Coombs sit in the scented blue homegrown haze of Meuenchau's Ford cab. I slide in, open a beer, take a hit. We share the threads of our bottom-of-the-world tapestry: back orders, a busted vat of lethal parts dip, Barry pinned with two ribs broken by a runaway pallet of Pennzoil. They're content with work, sleep, dope, and Jack in the Box. They have no fear or thought of dying and leaving nothing. Time is a sort of funny, irrelevant gas. Marijuana supplants the need for sex. Myself, I've got work to do, dreams to cash in. I can't derail again. Even high, I know I'm running out of time. Pretty soon I'm going to start that novel. Martin Eden, here I come. See you bright and early in the morning, fellows.

About this time, Javier Medina, a heroin addict with federal pen time and gang activity also on his résumé, makes a surprising reappearance. I never thought I'd see him again. It's been five years since he disappeared. But the news is that he's kicked. And he wants to start over and reenter this dispiriting suburban theater we call normal society. I have to say he looks good, like the old Javier, the track star, the varsity basketball player. And he's got a tag-along heavyset Boston honey named Flora with messed-up teeth who seems homey and solid, the kind of maternal influence a guy teetering on the precipice might need. And I've always liked Javier. He has a nimble mind; he's a fountain of jokes and quaint expressions. I've soiled my garments! he cries. Or in a barker's patter: What's the difference between an epileptic oyster shucker and a prostitute with diarrhea? Standing over a charcoal grill he twirls his spatula and announces: If it's smokin' it's cookin', if it's burnin' it's done! He can quote Tom Waits by the ream. And though he appears to be a hard case, the sort of gnarled chap you'd expect to see snarling in a federal cage, squat with long arms, scarred hooked nose, that dark humor of Mayan rage in his eyes (and he's so quick no one around here even thinks about fooling with him), I've never had a reason to dislike or distrust him.

All Javier needs now, besides the power to resist, is a job. Not an easy task for an ex-heroin addict with a criminal record who hasn't worked officially in three or four years. But the answer of course is the chemical warehouse. They're always hiring. I put in a good word for him. Whether or not I've done him a favor, Javier is hired.

Javier throws himself into his work up there on the Fram deck all alone, works like an ox filling jobber crates with oil, air, and fuel filters. It's hot and dusty up there. I started there myself. But there's a satisfaction in working alone, in having the territory to yourself, and the work, at least weight wise, is pretty light. I christen him the Sheriff of Fram County, warn him of the rattlesnakes and the cold winters up there, the wild Indians and porcupines.

I don't see Meuenchau and Coombs much anymore. They've moved out of the truck and spend their evenings indoors in the Medina home, an easier place to keep your beer cold, flat well-lit surfaces to roll your doobies, an address to have a pizza delivered, better speakers for your Moody Blues, and so on. Worries me a bit that they might be a bad influence on Javier, but Javier will have to weather stronger temptations than this, and he has known these boys all his life. He's exactly Meuenchau's age. They went to school together every grade, until Meuenchau fell behind and then eventually quit. I understand also that a little pot is probably a good thing. A man who kicks by himself, without methadone or 12-step or a personal safari guide through the oozing poppy forest, the man who can assert the staunchest independence, not only against addictive compounds but also against the social institutions that turn us to addictive compounds in the first place, actually has a better statistical chance in the long run of staying chemically independent. As long as a needle doesn't appear, what's wrong with a little party? No one is telling the ex-junkie that he must wear a straightjacket and sit on a wooden pew reciting flower names for the rest of his life.

Meuenchau and Coombs seem to be improved by their new relationship with our resurrected comrade. They seem more intent, hardworking, focused, less trivial. Though they are smoking more, and seem suddenly concerned about such matters as the new shipping and receiving table and whether or not the NAPA order goes out on time, and even though they might be a little rushed and even agitated at times, I find the change if not refreshing, then at least interesting. I'm ignoring some obvious signals: the dilated pupils, grinding jaw muscles, constant sniffing, and those faraway looks like men in death-row card games (note also that Coombs's Tourette's symptoms have all but disappeared, and Meuenchau, as practically sexless as they come, has begun seriously talking about girls), but since I don't see them much anymore, I'm convinced that their new indoor life, perhaps some of Mama Flora's navy beans with ham and homemade Boston cream pie, and the model progress of Javier, has inspired them to some sort of temporary self-motivation.

After work one night I stroll down to the Medina house, open the gate, appease the affable golden pound-dogs Pancho and Claude, and knock on the door. Flora answers, her eyes lucent, her chin thrust aerodynamically forward. Highly animated, a feather duster in her right hand, she seems flushed from exertion. By her reaction to me I might be her missing millionaire uncle. Hey man, she pants, shaking the feather duster at me. Come on in.

Oh, a party. Hello, everyone. Get him a beer, Flora. I ease into the living room. Javier is drawn up barefoot in his recliner singing along with Dan Hicks, "I Scare Myself." Coombs, leaned intently over the coffee table, is slowly tearing the pages from a hot rod magazine. Meuenchau, smoking stoically in the rocking chair, might be the Polish Marlboro Man. Flatmo, whom I went to high school with, stands in the corner in a leather jacket, long flat black hair sliced down the middle, a shimmer on his boots, jabbering intently with a girl I've never seen who has the ring-eyed aspect of a bandit. Flora has resumed her dusting of the hearth. Against the wall below a paint-by-numbers Blue Boy sits a nice-looking girl, daffodil hair, serenely satin gray eyes, looks like Dawn Fairburn from long ago. It is Dawn Fairburn. My word, what are you doing here?

I've known Dawn since the second grade. She and I were much alike, scurvy outside children who scored high on tests and tried to pretend we weren't smart so the other kids would like us. We almost went steady in fifth grade. Dawn had a bad skin problem, which insured her rejection by the Allied Powers of Popularity. Then long about ninth grade she blossomed into Brigitte Bardot and left us all in the dust. The last time I saw her was at the Strand, the movie theater in Ocean Beach, though she barely acknowledged me, so lustrous and thronged with admirers was she. I heard that she married the high school QB. I have a look around and wonder where Young Roy might be.

Presently there's a *clack clack clack* and Flatmo, emerged from his frothy *entre nous* with the bandit girl, taps the razor one last time and is handing a mirror to Meuenchau. The guests lean in as if Pavlov has rung a bell. Meuenchau is all business, head tipped suddenly back, nostril clamped. Blood seems to fill his left eye. The silver platter floats to the next hand. Bowed heads jerk up with muffled anguish and then silent blinking at the ceiling, like some kind of devotional rite.

When the mirror comes around to me I stare into the smeared lines. I'd really thought that, like smallpox and polio, this stuff had been expunged from the planet. In all the places I've been in the last ten years I haven't seen it or even heard it mentioned except by a pair of black-toothed biker-losers who were using it intravenously. A few vague memories trickle back through a general sense of misgiving. Dawn smiles at me, long lost beautiful Dawn with those uplifted Swedish eyes, the pleasant undulant mouth, the legs she knows just how to cross. The look says to me: Go home if you want, you'd be stupid to stay, but of course if you do stay there are many things I'd like to tell you. Besides, it's Friday. I realize she probably needs amateur psychological help. You can't be doing lines of crystal meth alone in the house of an ex-junkie if you're happily married. I wonder if she remembers that time on the playground of Grover Cleveland Elementary when we were flying homemade kites after school. All the other kids had left, and I was thinking about asking her to go steady with me. She seemed to be waiting for me to ask her to go steady, too, but I never did.

One line certainly won't hurt, I think, and the gifted artist among his less-gifted peers cannot be a sissy pants down on the wharf. I bend to the task. Whoosh comes the flying insect killer up into my cranium, the caustic eye-watering flames, the feeling that I will bleed or go blind. It's crank all right, the same blistering pestilence the PSA mechanic gave me when I was fifteen, changed in name only. Coombs to my right, restless as a cat, hunches over the mirror and rips whatever's left off the glass, then fingers the corners and rubs his gums, as if the stuff is coke. I'd chide him, but it doesn't matter, does it? Sniffing back bitter drops, I'm at ease for the first time in years. I'd forgotten this part: the stuff works on me—the same way it diffuses the majority of Coombs's motor tics, praxias, and lalias—like Ritalin (trade name for central nervous system stimulant methylphenidate) works on hyperactive children. I can't explain how but it slows us both down somehow.

Overall the effect of this inhaled form of industrial-strength speed is Pentecostal Church Meets Hercules at the Beach. There's a feeling like love, galactic in its proportions, blend in fulfillment, well-being, and above all potency, the sense that if you wanted to you could do anything: finish a novel, write a symphony, spin the couch with two people on it like a basketball on your fingertip, wallpaper the living room, find a girl, settle down and have a family, drive on up to Canada and sell all the belts you just tooled, anything, it's just that you choose instead to stay here and talk with these wonderful people who share your dreams, who are as loving and optimistic as you because after all they are your family. And the stuff isn't like cocaine, it costs nothing and lasts for hours, days if you want; you're not chained with a bunch of blithering bootlicking snufflers to endless hundred-dollar packets scared to death of tumbling off your high at any minute.

With robust leisure we devour the powder from the carousel mirror. I feel like Sir Isaac Newton after seventeen cups of coffee. I am immortal and indestructible. While Coombs and Meuenchau arm wrestle at the coffee table and Flora cleans behind the stove (say what you like about the scourge of methamphetamine in America but look at all the spotless kitchens!) I chain-smoke, play Ping Pong and foosball in the garage, listen to records, speak authoritatively on all subjects, make jokes, play darts, and play cards. I drink a case of beer, which has the same effect as water. Flatmo, the dealer, is cutting this stuff out free because he's rich. That's his BMW out front. Flatmo is another shining example of the nobody transported to the royal ball by the fairy meth-mother, although in this version he snorts the glass slipper, and the only prince in the story are the finger-prince the police take when he's busted (first time suspended sentence, second time three-and-a-half years federal time). Until then he can have three girls a night, four if he wants, take them all in a Lear jet to Newfoundland in the morning. Women love meth more than men (I mean that both ways), power and escape plus all the supermarket magazine promises: energy, weight loss (take thirty pounds off your fanny!), improved self-esteem, and increased sexual stamina.

Finally Dawn and I are out on the patio, cigarettes burning in our fingers. In her petite summer dress she's the poster girl for adolescent fascination: bronze legs, gold hair falling like coins, that sulky bottom lip, those inquisitive brows (or brows that seem to say: Wouldn't you like to know me a little better?). You know, I've actually never talked to her except in the most modest of exchanges. She's not exactly what I thought she'd be: she says "ain't" and "don't" for "isn't" and "doesn't," the way most of these sons and daughters of machinists, punch press operators, navy captains, and firemen of this neighborhood speak. That's the way I speak, too. We can't betray our class, can't appear to be snobs. She's smart though, knows the difference between the famous German movie director and the novel by Saul Bellow. I wonder, as I regard the luxuriance of that mouth, the glacial glimmer of those eyes, how she squandered her chance, why she isn't studying international business at UCSD. I mean, you're permitted to leave this neighborhood and become successful, just, when you come back, don't forget to say ain't and don't.

Her marriage has been dead for some time, she explains. A mistake to marry so young, to select such an obvious candidate, a man on his wedding day already slipping from his greatest achievement. Yes, he had scholarship offers from Cal and Utah State, but he never even replied. The aging newlyweds are kind of messed up on meth, she admits, but on his party days he likes to hang with the boys, play darts for a weekend, go fishing and fall out of the boat, sizzle a football through the leprous mist and talk about that game against Lincoln when they were down by seventeen but came back to win it on a sixty-yard option with no time on the clock. And he's probably sleeping with someone else. They stay together because it's convenient, she says, because they don't have that much money, because they don't want to distress family members who are already perplexed by Ken and Barbie on the Rocks, and because, in the diminishing middle of the constantly divided sum, they don't know what else to do.

Not having seen meth in long-sequence action yet, I assume that she describes a phase. It is a hard time in our mid-twenties when we realize that we are not going to be movie stars, acclaimed best sellers, or famous athletes as our childhood fantasies and our millions of hours of television watching dictated. Likely she assumed her captivating features would land her in a Breck ad or a Roman Polanski film, not the living room of an ex-heroin addict. I tell her I'm working on a novel. She says she plans on going back to school soon to get her teaching credentials. Our dreams seem not only accessible, close enough to touch, but also completed. But it's true, isn't it? I mean if I weren't out here (bladder swelling) leaning against the brick and chattering with this jelly nougat from my past I'd go home right now and type it up, be done with it, mail it off tomorrow.

GOD STRIKE ME with a urine-soaked newspaper if I ever do this drug again, the aftermath is simply unforgiving, a hangover infinitely more excruciating than alcohol, as if your nerves have been shaved by an asthmatic witch doctor, pumped with mustard gas, and then stomped crookedly by a drunken plumber who refuses to scrape his boots. Unlike coke or heroin, there is nothing whatsoever subtle or romantic about this souped-up bathtub solvent concocted from the very items I move daily at the chemical warehouse. I'm convinced that methamphetamine is not a drug but a plague, which I believe Nature, in order to keep her mortal quota, has supplied in lieu of yellow fever and cholera. Think of all the great heroin songs, from "MacArthur Park," to the Beatles' "Happiness Is a Warm Gun," to "China Girl" by David Bowie and "Voodoo" by Godsmack ("God Smack" is also a heroin song by Alice in Chains). There have to be as many great cocaine songs (from Cab Calloway to J. J. Cale to System of a Down), but there are good reasons no one writes great songs about meth:

the same reasons no one writes songs about yellow fever and cholera.

I am back at Javier's the next Friday. Amphetamines can be useful, I tell myself, a creative dynamo even. Think of Bob Fosse and Ayn Rand. For five years I was Howard Roark, the uncompromising architect hero in *The Fountainhead*, a novel that Rand wrote on amphetamines. And don't you fret, if Ayn Rand can do it, I can too. My drugs are about twenty times stronger than hers.

Javier, Meuenchau, Coombs, Flora, and I begin another two-and-a-half-day binge, which starts the moment we leave work on Friday afternoon. We stop and get plenty of cigarettes and beer. We take measures for reinforcements. I make provisions to visit my parents and appear to have slept. Like Nazis and religious fanatics, we escape into power. As many as twenty revelers might flow in and out of this Fiesta of the Damned, every one blighted, greasy, sniffing, febrile, ashen, chattering, molars wearing down, arteries hardening, heart straining, brain wavering, even though the luminous diabolical deception inside, despite the overwhelming evidence to the contrary, refuses to yield.

Parties for me have always been events where inebriation was requisite to relaxation, but now with the meth I am the Effortless Me, amiable, witty, vibrant. As Dawn's marriage continues to crumble, my prayers are answered and soon she is a weekend regular too. She and I find excuses to take walks, to chat on the patio. We volunteer for liquor-store runs. We seem to have the most in common, or perhaps that is only another way of saying the most to lose. We fizzle into Sunday evening like the dead returning to Gomorrah.

Before long I'm frightened by these weekly binges, these accursed cycles against my will, these destructive cravings that have supplanted the fragile existence of everything I stand for: art and independence and the pleasure of family, evenly paced conversation, scratch cookin', and sleeping in on Sunday morning. I'm starting to look sickly. The excitement I once reserved for my novel and women is now spent on the drug-binge release and my blathering camaraderie. My head swarms with shadows and black flies. My novel and future have dissolved like the toxic dust in my lungs. Each time I peek over the ledge of that mirror heaped with oily piles of crystalline misery I try not to see the ravaged man with the inflamed nostrils and the leaden, greedy eyes.

Dawn likes that vegetarian restaurant on University Avenue that serves the edible flowers. Her favorite song is Joan Baez's "Diamonds and Rust." She jokes about becoming a stripper to pay the bills. It's not unusual to be walking along with her and look over to see her climbing a tree. She has those streaks of down that run catlike from her jawline to the nape of her exquisite neck. We slip away when we can to the Ken Cinema, a revival movie house in Kensington, to watch old French movies, anything black and white with children running through fields of poppies. Next door is the Club Kensington, a mandatory cocktail lounge (well, aren't they all?) where one night on the TV there's a document-ary about Jim Jones, the charismatic religious leader and former door-to-door monkey salesman who drew his followers to the jungles of Guyana and induced a mass suicide with cyanide-spiked Kool-Aid , who unwittingly sponsors the documentary. (Actually Jones used Flavor Aid, but since few know Flavor Aid, the Kool-Aid legend is now secure, so much so that the popular phrase "drink the Kool-Aid," meaning a commitment of unwav-ering loyalty, derives from this event.) The delectable absurdity of Kool-Aid as a sponsor to a Jim Jones documentary combined with the depth of people more lost and self-destructive than we are makes us laugh so hard that we must hold on to each other, a moment in which I realize I would rather die than miss a chance with her.

Later that night on the beach we stroll the hard wet sand along the edge of the last skimming waves. The thick fog smells of chewable vitamins and prehistoric fish. The flicker-haunted surf has its own natural babble and chant. A yellow glow as we approach a lamp outlines the shape of a figure slumped in a wheelchair along the boardwalk. The scent of wet charcoal drifts up from a fire pit. Without a word we stop and face each other. We can't, I say. That's supposed to be my line, she says. I'm leaving soon, I mumble. All the better, she says. I'll have to change the name of my novel to *I Am a Varmint*, I say. Fuddy-duddy, she says, taking my hand, and we stroll back down into the sea-roaring darkness.

Three days later by the pool table at a retirement bar at seven in the morning, she presses up against me in a muscular feline arch and plants a big long kiss on me. We're haggard and wasted with scarecrow hair. Our brains are syrup. We're running on polluted tertiary neural residue and cheap draft beer. Clouds in my head, I think for a moment about ravishing her on the green felt right in front of these goopy-eyed pensioners in their Goodwill hats, then remind myself where it will lead (would I want the star QB to shoot my wife into the corner pocket?). I wonder how long I will keep falling and if Dawn will follow me to the end. I refresh myself with scenes from the window of a Greyhound bus. Too bad I only have sixteen bucks.

Though Coombs's Tourette's symptoms have diminished, they've been replaced by a more sinister set of signs. He has, for example, stopped going to work half the time. We drive by to pick him up and he's still in bed, sick he says. (Sick is right.) As he sits smoking or contemplating, his brain a-humming, he digs at raw patches on his scalp where the hair is falling away. Also, he's begun to discuss in detail the prophecies of Nostradamus and Edgar Cayce. Once a simple, playful soul, he's inherited the dark burden of a goofed-up planet trapped in time. He's worrisome, not fun. He's a self-medicated, self-made, bloody-headed spook. Aren't you concerned about your liver, man, I ask him, your heart, your brain? I don't think about things that way, he answers. And when he has to spend a weekend in observation because his Edgar Cayce infatuations have gotten too real, no one goes down to visit him. Frankly we're a bit afraid, as if we might be waddling downtown to witness our own future. Anyway, he'll be all right. He just has to lay off the powder awhile, which he doesn't.

The once plump Flora, like many women under the thrall of monster-truck amphetamines, thinks her emaciation somehow appealing. When she learns that she is pregnant, however, she leaves immediately for Boston, knowing a child would stand little chance of survival in our roller coaster off its tracks. Javier replaces her with a much more attractive, less house-cleaning-oriented girl named Brenda, courtesy of Flatmo, and no one thinks much about Flora anymore. We don't miss her at all, especially Javier.

Meuenchau is having gum problems and suspects that his teeth are falling out. He has begun to date a sixteen-year-old girl known affectionately and salaciously around the neighborhood as "Da Beef," also a chronic meth user, though she leaves him to marry another much older man across town (who, by coincidence, is a meth dealer), and Meuenchau, distraught and crying, locks himself in the Medina bathroom, refusing to come out. I wonder if he will cut his wrists or try to flush himself down the toilet. We think we might have to call someone, who? His mother perhaps? At last, after I confess to him seven rousing romantic failures (plenty more where that came from), he comes out mopping his eyes with his bony wrists and vows to quit drugs. Consider that snooze-bar life Meuenchau had before meth: slow smiling dreamy shake hands with everyone, watching the same *Twilight Zone* episode over and over because he doesn't remember it, catching a big glittering fish on Sunday now Mama with roast beef on the table scattered like sheep shit in the hot Wyoming wind. Yes, he's going to quit these stupid fucking drugs, go back to the gentle life where he can keep his teeth awhile longer, he says, though he doesn't quite make it.

Javier and I are the only ones who make it to work every day now. Granitelike as Javier seems, he startles me sometimes because he appears to be shrinking, his face is turning to vellum, his hair is patched with gray. The smirk on his little-old-man

face seems to suggest that his premature decay is not only inten-
tional, but somehow funny. I wonder how anyone can volunteer
for a meaningless death so young. I don't include myself in this,
you see, because I'm going to quit these drugs any day now.
I really mean it this time.

I don't know how many weeks or months have gone by, but
it's Sunday night and Dawn's got to get home. She hasn't called
her husband in two or three days. Doesn't know if he's been out
all week partying, moved to Idaho, filed for divorce, sold the
house, gone off on a jaunt to Vegas because he's heard LA Dodger
pitcher Bob Welch is signing cards at the Stardust, or died on
the rug from an overdose, but she must get home.

And I aim to get her there, see her safe, she's practically my
cousin: we have the same grammar-school blood in our veins,
the same unfinished dreams, the same coital resistance, the same
empty gift boxes littered across the floor, the same shame, the
same disbelief. She's starting to look rough, her teeth oxidized,
her hair desiccating; she's skinny not thin; her nice little ass
has shrunk to two apples in a cloth bag; her once luminous skin is
fading; glass-crack wrinkles are spreading from the corners of
her eyes. She's looking less like Brigitte Bardot and more like
Ernest Hemingway every day. But do you think I care? My love is
a loyal love, an indestructible superpower love (drink the Kool-
Aid!): you know if we'd gone steady in the fifth grade none of this
probably would've ever happened…

Quacking and waddling, grinding and blinking away, we
approach her house. It must be four in the morning, dead quiet,
cool autumn verging on winter, moths tumbling around the
lamps. He must be asleep, I say. Come inside, she says, reaching
down to take my hand. I squeeze her fingers. The house is dark
and smells sepulchral with loneliness. Young Roy is not dead, not
here anyway.

Dawn and I are still holding hands. Let's screw, she says.
Christ, I thought it would be different somehow. OK, I say. Where?
The guest room, she says. We sneak down the hall. The guest

room has a bunny theme, a sewing machine, at least not a reaping machine. We kiss hotly with much tongue. She's not for foreplay, ripping open my jeans, pulling my T-shirt over my head. I take down her costume and we kiss naked. She's still wearing her socks. She's very agile, not a shy girl, strong too, even if she's lost twelve pounds in the last four months, hasn't eaten for two days, her eyes hollowing in their sockets.

Amphetamine has the largely fraudulent reputation of a performance enhancer, but lust is the one real pleasure left to us, the one desire not totally supplanted by endorphins, we attack as if unleashing twelve Hoover Dam turbines. I believe we're also exercising a form of desperation, the shoveling over of emptiness, the heated lunging chase after that answer beyond our grasp, but we leap across each other like chattering jackrabbits. Headboard clapping against the wall, the bed seems to swing, the sky seems to spin. This should've been my girl, I think. This should be my dream come true. I let go and listen for the front door. She reaches up to kiss me, eyes aglitter, and says, "Where were you when I was thirteen?"

Now with my "need" for Dawn the weekends have an added demon riding upon the serpent's neck. We slip away, sneak off, staggering departures, we leave early, make an excuse, find union in a car, in a park, on the cement pad behind the liquor store. Once we have it out in the dawn's early light of some kind of ridiculous leafless bush. Every effect of this graceless union conspires to make me ill. But this drug drives me to frenzy, pushes every last raw sin to the tips of my tensile nerves. I'm electric with desire. I'm a boulder of a cock. She's a lake of wetness, arched up, watching me slide into her, her front teeth pushed forward, her eyes switched off. And then we're whamming and slamming, and she's moaning so loud I have to cover her mouth. I wonder what we must look like crashing into each other, two skinny blue apes, two corpses. I want to get this over with. The sky is red with the rising sun. I'm not going to do this again. Is that all I ever say? But I'm not. I'm going to run away. I'm going to go someplace where no one will find me. I know I will be the same person, but I'll run again, and then eventually I'll get old and desire will fade and then I can live in peace.

My reprieve comes in the form of a phone call in February. An old friend I cooked with in Colorado has just graduated from the Culinary Institute of America in Hyde Park and has landed his first job as a chef in the dying city of Niagara Falls, New York. He can't find any decent cooks. Would I like to come out and help him? If I could reach down through the phone wires I would hug him. He has no idea how he has saved me, though of course he hasn't.

One last night together, drunk and cranked up (the last time, I really mean it), Dawn and I drive down the interstate to Ocean Beach. We're such a rangy spluttering ratty old couple, I hope a cop doesn't pull us over and think we've escaped from a hospital or missed the boat to Guyana. As usual, I'm flummoxed as to why we could not have met under normal circumstances, why this cannot be righted somehow: the impenetrable nature of my cheating, burning, dying life, this notion of a diamond of art in the vault of hell, and these torrid souls I always find to clutch in my descent.

It's cold at the beach, drizzling, so we sit in the car in a lot overlooking Sunset Cliffs. In seven hours with another ripping hangover I'll be looking down from a plane window onto a dead city encased in ice. But at least they won't have meth in Niagara Falls, not for about two years anyway. And for a month or two, I'll read classics on the floor of my ancient unfurnished apartment by the radiator and I'll fly straight, regain a rickety order, take careful notes, drink tea, steam the windows with my deep thoughts, and pretend to be mistreated, unlucky, and misunderstood until boredom, lust, and the New Flatmos come gather me up for another graveyard waltz.

Dawn clings to me, her gaunt eyes vexed and wet, the windows fogged. On the radio there is a Blind Faith song, "Can't Find My Way Home." What I should suggest to this rare creature of my affection is that we make some kind of pact, use our brains to dig each other out of this pit. We're too young to decay. We'll clean up, comb our hair, and see if we can't find that door to adulthood. I'll finish my novel; you return to school. But you'll see that every time I call it love it's really something else: the married woman, the troubled girl, the one I meet just before it's time to go, each doomed arrangement a carefully selected guarantee of pleasure and the unimpeded escape.

Dawn kisses me violently, panic in her eyes. I'll come with you, she says. Yes, I say vaguely, but it seems to me that, like Coombs, Meuenchau, and Javier, she's not going to quit until her heart stops or someone takes her away and puts her into a room against her will. And I've got enough problems of my own. Dawn is breaking down now—she won't let go of my neck. If it wasn't a lie I'd tell her everything is going to be all right. I have to go, Dawn, I say gently, and as she looks up, all I can see is that skinny, fifth-grade girl all alone on an elementary school playground, flying that homemade kite.

Conspiracy and Apocalypse
at the McDonald's
in Goodland, Kansas

I LEFT ENCINITAS, CALIFORNIA, APRIL 1, 1997, WITH
five hundred dollars in traveler's checks, four hundred dollars in
twenty-dollar bills folded into the secret pocket of my jacket, and
sixty dollars in my front left pocket. I do this in case I get robbed.
Spread your cash. If someone robs you, give him the smallest
parcel. If the shithead persists, offer the traveler's checks. I have
been robbed twice, once at knifepoint, once at gunpoint. No
one ever wanted the traveler's checks.

The bus ticket was fifty-nine dollars: anywhere in the country, three weeks advance. I bought a ticket for Odessa, Texas.
I had never been to Odessa before. Well, I had passed by the outskirts once, seen a motel along the highway for $11.95 a night.
The town had looked like a miserable place where people
wouldn't want to go, which is the criterion I have used to pick my
travel destinations for the last ten years. I have been to all the
places where people want to go, and those are the worst places
to live: they are crowded, the rent and the crime are high,
the competition for pastries is fierce, and there is often a rude
or exclusive attitude. In places no one wants to go, the rent
is cheap, the people are happy to see a stranger (what are you
doing here?), and it's usually pretty easy to get a job—so it's
upside-down logic, but not really. People on the bus are always
disappointed, though, when I tell them I am going to Rhode
Island or New Jersey or Nebraska or Arkansas. They want you to
say Florida or Colorado.

So anyway, I had a ticket for Odessa and a little less than a thousand dollars. I also had six San Francisco sourdough rolls— three stuffed with kosher beef salami, onions, and mustard, and three with cream cheese sprinkled with crushed red pepper. I'd never done that before, the crushed red pepper. It was just a whim, an instinct almost. I thought of jalapeño peppers first, but there were no jalapeños around. The crushed red worked out pretty well. I was pleasantly surprised.

I like to have a thousand dollars when I land in a new place, but I have landed with a lot less: eighty-five once in Colorado Springs; forty one winter in New Orleans; two hundred when I made the catastrophic tropical island trek. Even a grand goes fast. Say you stay at a motel two or three nights, but the ketchup factory isn't hiring or you can't find a place to live or there are too many parking meters downtown or the people are grouchy or whatever, so you don't want to stay. The motel is seventy or eighty; the ticket out is fifty or sixty. Throw in the food you ate, the beer you drank, the paperback you bought, and you've spent $150 in three days. Do this three times and when you finally find the right spot you won't have enough for a room and deposit and spending money to last until you get a job. You will have a nickel in your pocket and you will rattle it around in there and think, Why didn't I just stay in the last place? This time I wanted to get to someplace and have enough so I could coast awhile and not have to take the first crummy job that came along. Then maybe I'd save enough to quit through the winter, watch the snow and scratch my toes and read the *Summa Theologica* and all the novels of Alexandre Dumas.

I rode the bus for two days and one night. A skinny-legged girl in silver vinyl sat next to me, staring off into space and breaking out occasionally into bright grins and now and then cupping hand to mouth to suppress an irresistible giggle. I was sure she was either tripping or insane. Or there may have been some laughing gas leaking down in an isolated current from one of the baggage compartments. Behind me sat a potbellied epicurean truck driver who'd just dropped off his rig in Bakersfield and was headed to Phoenix and who talked to his neighbor in an even, agreeable, gravelly voice about food: "I like chiles rellenos," he graveled. "I like crab, Dungeness crab from Louisiana, boiled in beer with lemon juice. I like crab better than lobster. Lobster's too sweet. I like sausages, the kind with the casing on it. You cook it and the casing splits and it's juicy. I like halibut broiled with vinegar and garlic, but also baked and fried. I like all kinds of Mexican food, especially sausage. Have you had the chorizo? Steak is my favorite, though. I like chicken breaded in butter-milk and cracker crumbs and fried..." He went on like this for hundreds of miles. I have cooked in eighteen different kitchens, but he knew more about cooking than I did (although I do know Dungeness crab is not from Louisiana). He made me hungry. I had to eat one of my kosher-salami sandwiches. Finally he got off the topic of food and uttered a utilitarian maxim about life that is the closest thing to the truth behind the mystery that I have ever heard; he said it confidently and with comforting humor to a listener who was apparently having a hard time of it: "Things go up and things go down," he said. "It's as simple as that." He got off in Phoenix and asked the bus driver what had happened to the old depot. The driver was happy that he had asked about the old depot.

Standing in line at the new depot in Phoenix, waiting for a connection, I met another gravel-voiced stranger, a gay biker. He wore a black leather vest, leather biking cap, and gray frosted sunglasses. He was fat and heavily tattooed, with a porous candle-wax complexion. He had a rough Chicago accent. He'd been a cop in Chicago until some drunk had run him down and broken both his hips. When they sent him to Tucson to convalesce, he'd discovered he was gay. At one time he'd been married. He'd just seen his children in Flagstaff, but it was too cold in Flagstaff and he'd left a day early. The cold made his heart hurt, he explained, and then he lifted his shirt to show me his elephant-belly scars and talked modern heart-surgery lingo; he'd had a double bypass, then a triple. "There will be no next surgery," he graveled glamorously. "I've already told my kids to bury me with my '61 Harley and a carton of Camel unfiltereds." He was going to the Gay Olympics in Amsterdam in 1998. He worked on the Olympic Committee. He told me he'd just won $17,500 on a bet he'd made in the Arizona-Kentucky game, but he didn't know enough about gambling to make me believe it. I was glad to see him get on another bus. Anybody who just won $17,500 on a college-basket-ball wager ought to be able to at least afford a plane ticket.

Now that we were in proximity again to the vast population centers, the bus was crowded. I sat up front. In the back next to the bathroom sit the all-night yakkers whose mouths swing end-lessly open and shut like the bathroom door. They are young and on parole and their uncle has kicked them out of the house and they know the complete Star Wars trilogy by heart and have to get out at every stop for a smoke. I used to sit back there myself, as far away from Papa Driver as possible, where you can snicker and take sleeping pills and nip from a bottle of Four Roses and maybe get the butter from a slutty young road queen. A Mexican sat next to me, stoic and polished dark as wood, white straw hat, neat trimmed mustache, bag at his feet. I had my bag at my feet, too. And my sandwiches were good. I made them last two days. The cream cheese holds up better than you would think, especially sprinkled with crushed red pepper. I also had a bag of trail mix and a PowerBar, which tastes pasty and mealy, like algae and sunflower seeds and sterile honey from a nunnery, but it's good for you, so don't worry. Have your PowerBar.

I never read on the bus. I don't even bother bringing a book. I don't talk either; why make a fool of myself? Hey, where you going? This is what I think about God and the president. Who cares? My favorite thing in the world is to do nothing. Sitting on a bus, especially when the seat next to you is empty, you can just glide along, look out the window. I don't care if there is no scen-ery. I hope there is no scenery. I will sit and look out the windows and feel the motion of the bus and maybe if I'm woozy take a

Dramamine—which makes me drowsy, which together must be droozy, or wowsy, no, droozy it is—and think my half-assed thoughts. The sky is a big drive-in screen with the clouds of my life floating across it. I figured it all out long ago. But it doesn't matter if you figure it out or not. We all end up at the same place eventually. The rivers run into the sea and the sea is never filled. So I do nothing. Stare out the window. Go with the rhythm. Be in the now of the Greyhound. Get off in the little windy spots with the convenience stores and the other passengers squinting and sucking on their low-tar butts, maybe getting a pop or a big bag of red-hot pork rinds or nacho-cheese Doritos to bring back on the bus. Dragging their children by the arm, bewildered children in overalls with sleep in their eyes. But brave children who think their parents know where they are going. Their mother, I mean. The father is not around, usually. If he were, he would drive them in his big pickup truck, because with the child support and the drunk-driving charge he doesn't have enough for a plane ticket. And chances are he isn't working anyway.

And all the way across the country the people are saying to themselves, I am never going to take the bus again as long as I live, and trying to sleep with their neck crooked and a book on their lap, their jacket rolled up, their face smooshed into the cold glass, trying to sleep next to the insane woman who thinks people are taking infrared pictures of her baby, a strange baby with long hands, almost newborn. But the mother is crazy, gets out at the little windy convenience-store places in the cold dark and smokes, holding her baby and glaring at the people who are taking infrared pictures of it, passing the pictures around, laughing at her. And she begins to swear at the people. She is foul-mouthed. Then she excuses herself for being rude. Then she shouts for the bus driver to stop these people from taking pit-chers of her baby, passing the pitchers around. She demands that this man be taken off the bus. He is the one. Either this man is taken off the bus, or she will leave. It's him or her (there is big support for letting her go). "Stop this bus!" she cries in the middle of cold nowhere, not even the yellow windows of houses, not even traffic signs, only the whisper of tumbleweeds and the sound of the wind blowing over her smooth hard mind.

And by morning we are all exhausted with her. The bus trip is enough. The little baby cries and cries. Finally she flounces up in a whirl, almost gets into a fight, and demands to be let off the bus. The driver relents, dropping her off at a McDonald's in some flyspeck of a town. She stalks away with her tiny white long-fingered newborn and people cackle after her, someone with more problems than them. They cackle about the pitchers and who's got the pitchers and, boy, are we glad that old weird poor insane hag of a woman is out of our hair, and all the time thinking about the little baby and what it will be like for that little helpless baby to have a mother who is insane, who is walking in the cold through a Texas town she has probably never seen before. And then we all start to feel bad. You can feel it running right down the bus like a current, humans poor and out of luck and tired, on our way to who knows where, and what will we do when we get there, but we are one for a while, thinking about that poor baby and the life it will have. And she's off wandering the streets of some damn strange town in Texas.

I watched the mother before all this started, in the Amarillo depot, where the buses were crammed and the waits were long and the drivers and baggage men and clerks were all absurdly holding it together, like the Romans after the first wave of Goths, as the depot swelled and the biofeedback machine (which also gave astrological readouts) inanely blinked. And of all the rough-edged, desperate, burnt-out, deranged people, she looked to be one of the more solid types, taking good care of her child, not distracted by the characters surveying us with their hats cock-eyed or the unsupervisable children stampeding up and down the lobby or the hunkering cigarette smokers with their conspiratorial laughter—she seemed solid. I guess she was barely holding on.

But that was Amarillo, which was long after Odessa. I

didn't even have to get off the bus at Odessa. I knew it would be wrong. Just had the feeling. I said to myself, I'll get a bicycle, bicycle to work, the store, the post office, the laundry, the house of my understanding girlfriend with the red hair and the overbite who studies the backs of cake mixes, who apologizes a lot and is curious about the lives of movie stars and serial killers. But just a glimpse of that town in the afternoon, the massive grueling industrial medieval hulk of it, and I knew it was no good. These Texas towns—all Western towns for that matter, but especially Texas towns—sprawl as if land were despised and the more you used up, the better, with their long strung-out Fifth Streets and monster-long Maple Streets with no maples, only juniper bushes and lawn mower shops and frozen yogurt and nails and tans and videos and pizza and baseball cards and motels and burgers and on and on. Odessa is a town in Texas you don't even think of when someone says Texas. You don't think of it, period. Someone said to me once, "Odessa, the Armpit of the Lone Star State," and I said, "Yes, my kind of city," but looking out the bus window I didn't even need to get off to see that it was smoldering and pulsing with crime and anonymity and vacant lots and competitive fried-chicken franchises. And I thought, Why do I fool myself? Why do I pay fifty-nine dollars and go to a place I know will not work? And then summer comes and I am like a dead fly under a dusty bed for six months. Why do I do this?

But I had been frugal, had spent no money. OK, I splurged on a large chocolate shake, but that was later with the Mormon in Goodland. He talked Mormon while I sucked on the shake. He was firm in his beliefs, but he was not trying to proselytize me. There was just something, I think, about the way I stood next to the window and drank my shake. Maybe he had heard me talk to the young man riding next to me, who was bringing a water pipe back from Mexico to his uncle in Flint, Michigan, delivering it by hand, watching over it as if it were a religious artifact, carrying the bag on his knees so it didn't get broken. On a bus all the way from Mexico. For days. I couldn't help but have fun with this. So maybe the Mormon had overheard this and made a judgment about me. Daniel the Mormon from Australia, who preached apocalypse in the McDonald's in Goodland, Kansas. He preached the one-world-government-via-the-UN conspiracy. (Where does this idea come from?) He said the Mormon Church was in apostasy. He was certain that three of the people in the recent Heaven's Gate mass suicide were Mormon prophets, which fit into his exact scheme of apocalypse. (Everyone, it seems, has a vision of apocalypse.) He was going to Missouri, the Zion of Mormonism. Daniel had many thoughts, thoughts on government plots, history unfolding to a point where it would all come clear. A final revelation.

I enjoyed talking with Daniel. At least he cared. I've never talked with anyone who really knows much, but there's usually something there, and I put in my meager bit. I like Mormons. They make as much sense as anyone, and they don't have the same kind of social decay as the lukewarm and the nondenominational and the unreligious. The Catholics and the Jews and the Mormons are all good at social coherency. There is something to be said for this. I'd talked to Mormons a week before in Encinitas (which, incidentally, is only a few miles from Rancho Santa Fe, where the Heaven's Gate people snuggled on their ball caps, tossed back their black elixirs, and happily ushered their souls off to the UFO riding in the icy tail of the Hale-Bopp comet). There were four of them, elders in white shirts smiling and nodding. They gave me The Book of Mormon. Jesus in the Americas. A new revelation. The concept of constant revelation, which says that as we grow and become more capable of understanding, more will be revealed to us about God's work. There is not only an evolution of matter but also an evolution of spirit. Destination. Purpose. All these things. And a large chocolate shake in Goodland, Kansas.

But I'm jumping ahead. I had been frugal. Or had I? To buy a ticket to a place you should have known was wrong is not frugal. The next town up was Plainview. Maybe 150 miles. There were other towns, but the name of this one was right. A dull name. A place where no one would go. People are not flocking to northwest Texas. They go to the country-and-western Mecca of Austin, the job and cultural centers of Dallas and Houston, the warm gulf. They don't go northwest. So Plainview it was, population twenty-one thousand. I got off in Odessa and bought a ticket. The bus left right away, so I didn't have to waste money on a motel or a cab or a lonesome roast-beef dinner. I was glad to be moving again, and somewhat anxious about arriving. A new place always means serious work. Not fun. The room, the job, the scrupulous management of money. You have to be deft, delicate, be fleet on your feet, budget-minded, like the good housewife of the 1950s. But now, in the interim, it was a little like a brainless Florida vacation. No pressure. See the countryside. I had a margin of error. Only thirty dollars to Plainview. Not irreversible if it turned out to be a mistake. No one on the bus to Plainview. That was a good sign.

The last stop before Plainview was a two-hour late-afternoon layover in Lubbock, which is not exactly a welcoming kind of place. I'd thought I might get a paper, have a look at rentals and jobs, but Lubbock was brooding and dark, troubled by something. Too much technology maybe. Lubbock is the home of Texas Technological College, the Church of the Tool Worshipers. Technology gives us cancer and then we want technology to cure us. Technology is a big dog with glittering eyes chasing its tail in a long and complicated dream. Lubbock was a technology-haunted place. They even had a security guard patrolling the church across the street. Then again, the bus terminal is always in the worst part of town. The kind Greyhound executives have designed it this way so homeless people can have a place to use the bathroom and bum cigarettes and wander along the sidewalk muttering as if they are indigent travelers, which I suppose they are.

It was dark when the bus rolled into Plainview. I was the

only one to get off. The station was closed. I had seen a motel on
the way in, the Sands, so I got all my bags and walked back to it,
about a mile. On the way I tried to get a feel for the town, but it
was too dark. I saw an unlocked bicycle on a porch. Good sign.
Then I saw a house with an iron gate on the front door. Bad sign.
The town was long. It looked more like a town of fifty or sixty
thousand than twenty-one. I kept switching hands with the suitcase. I finally found the Sands, a semicrummy-but-really-no-
room-to-complain motel. $24.68 a night and cops in the parking
lot: tenant altercation. The state as Mom and Dad. I am trying
to get away from this sort of thing. I chatted with the young man
at the desk: Where can I get a paper? How's the economy? Etcet-
era. Then I stowed my junk in my room, a tired old room like an
emphysemic aunt, the water-stained ceiling tiles knocked askew,
blue and white curtains to match the orange-striped wallpaper.
I needed to shower and eat, but I wanted to get a feel for the town.
If it wasn't right I'd have to pick up and get out fast. Couldn't be
spending twenty-five a night dillydallying.

I walked down the main stretch, which went about sixteen
or seventeen blocks. Too spread out. Not a good place to live
without a car. The usual fast-food-and-RadioShack façade, plastic armature concealing the real town in a psychological
experiment to see how long it takes before people start killing
each other. The only thing that set it apart from any other place
in America was a ranching supply company called BAR-F,
except instead of a hyphen there was a tiny diamond between the
R and the F. How much thought had gone into this name I
couldn't guess. Also, I finally saw the famous Hale-Bopp comet,
streaking across the firmament, dragging the souls of the tool
worshipers behind it.

Back in my room, I read the Plainview Daily Herald and ate
a can of sardines in hot sauce and some potato rolls I'd bought
at a convenience store and a candy bar full of peanuts, which
kept falling in my lap. Rents were high. There were a few jobs I
thought I might look at: one cooking, one janitorial, one unspec-

ified with no experience required. The paper was foolishness. Like canned corn. Like folk music with an accordion solo. Like *The Carol Burnett Show*. Newspapers are not interested in reality. I read them and feel I'm reading about a different world in a different time where people have big ears and freckles and wet hair combed straight back and are always asking you to pull their finger. It isn't good storytelling, just superficial skits about pet topics, like the evils of tobacco and sex scandals and the untimely deaths of famous people. Is the stock market up or down? Is the princess coming to visit? You pay a quarter and then throw the thing out when you are done with it.

I felt bad all night, had nightmares. Maybe they were hot-sardine dreams. Maybe they were from reading the *Plainview Daily Herald*. I was nervous and didn't want to admit it. I didn't like this place, but then I wouldn't like any strange new place where I was running out of money unless it was heaven and they had free chocolate-covered cherries. I got up at six in the morning (checkout time was eleven) and it was raining. Heavy solid gray rain. Rain in northwest Texas is rare. I put on my rain suit and went for a walk to get a feel for the town in the daylight, but it began to rain harder. I returned to the motel and went back to bed. At eight it was still raining. At nine it was raining. At ten it was raining harder than ever. I watched it from the window, sweeping and knifing across the ground. First it rained one way, then it rained the other. Pretty soon it was raining both ways.

So I said the hell with it. I didn't want to pitch any more money into the sea. A town has to do something, open its arms a little, give you a break, do something other than rain, especially when the rent is too high and it doesn't look all that great in the first place. I decided to go to Great Bend, Kansas. I had seen it on the map and liked it because it was the right size and because it was a geographical anomaly on the plains, a town on the elbow of a river. Might be interesting.

I walked back to the bus station in the rain. There were two people in the station. The guy behind the counter looked up.

"What can I get for you?" he said.

"Ticket to Great Bend," I said.

"Don't go there anymore," he said. "I think we used to."

"Let me think a minute … How about Garden City then?" I didn't really want to go to Garden City (it sounded nice—a bad sign), but where else was I going to go, Idaho?

He wrote me out a ticket to Garden City.

"How big is Garden City?" I asked.

"Pretty big," he said. He pulled an atlas out from under the counter and opened it. "Yeah, pretty big. Like sixty thousand."

"Well, I want to go someplace that isn't too big, you know. I am fleeing social decay."

He smiled at me, interested, and lit up a cigarette. "This is the Bible Belt," he said.

"Yes, I know, but the rent is too high."

"They just opened two penitentiaries outside of town," he said. "Good jobs."

"And it's raining," I added.

"Yeah, it hardly ever rains here."

"I bring the rain with me, I think. Last two places I lived flooded out."

"Maybe you could hire yourself out to farmers."

"Rice farmers."

"You probably wouldn't like Garden City a whole lot."

"I want some dull little place where the people wave to you and the kids don't have to lock their bicycles at school and you don't read in the daily paper every day about how a torso was discovered in a dumpster and they don't even know who it belongs to."

He nodded along. He had read the Plainview Daily Herald, too. He was a friendly guy, and business was mighty slow because people don't travel to Plainview very often. He looked at the map. "How about Hays?" he said. "Hays is a nice town. I knew a girl once from Hays."

"How many people?"

He checked the atlas. "Seventeen thousand."

"That's about right," I said. "How much?"

"Eighty-nine."

"Sheezus." I had to think about that. "No, too high. I could go to Pennsylvania for that."

"I'll give it to you for seventy-one," he said.

I didn't know how he could arrange this. Maybe he was the owner and could work a senior discount for me or something. White-newborn-with-insane-mother rate. I thought a second, worked my tiny mind. I still like the way the town's name sounded when he pronounced it. Haze. "Sign me up," I said.

He scribbled out the ticket. "Bus leaves at 7:40 tonight."

It was eleven in the morning. I hadn't eaten yet, didn't have any food left in my bag. The rain was too heavy to walk anywhere. I sat down in one of the hard curved blue chairs. The rain would let up eventually. If God was going to end the world he probably wouldn't start in the Bible Belt.

But the rain didn't let up, and my companion had to close the place down from noon to two. He had to kick me out.

"Can I leave my luggage?"

"Leave it," he said.

I asked him where the nearest grocery store was, and he pointed and directed, and I put on my rain suit and headed out into it. The streets were awash and the red mud was thick and slick as I trudged along, thinking, I'd better get back soon before this son of a gun floods out. The store was about two miles. The gutters were so swollen I could hardly jump over them. A guy stopped to offer me a ride, swung open his door. I slipped in the mud, sank a little, leaned down to look in, smiled. "No, just killing time anyway," I said. And it was true. I had all day and nothing to do but get my shoes wet and slip around in the red northwest-Texas mud.

At the store I bought a bag of bagels, four bananas, two
cans of tuna in canola oil, one can of fish steaks with chilies, one
six-ounce square of cream cheese, box of Little Debbie brownies.
Enough food for three days. Total: $6.59. I stood out in front
of the store and watched the rain and ate two brownies, then a
banana, then a bagel, then another banana, then two more
brownies. This is important: a can of pork and beans is meaningful, a roof is meaningful, a job, doughnuts, friendly neighbors,
time—time is always meaningful. The struggle is missing from
most American lives. There is struggle but it is a struggle for
luxuries. I think of the little frontier girl delighted beyond all
bounds by a glass of lemonade or a stick of horehound candy.
This was me out in front of the grocery store in the rain with my
bananas and my Little Debbie's brownies that day. I could not
have been happier; I would not have asked to be anywhere else.

When I finally got back to the depot, my shoes and socks
were soaked through and I was splattered and dipped in the
Texas red mud, so I changed my shoes and socks and wiped off
my rain suit and hung everything over the back of a chair to
dry, and felt pretty good. The rain kept coming. I watched it come
down. The cars hissed and sloshed by. I felt the emptiness of
the depot and longed for a smoke. There were no people coming
or going because there was only one bus out and that was the
7:40, my bus. The guy at the counter smoked cigarettes, read the
paper, listened to the radio—a talk show. Some caller didn't
want to pay his taxes because the money went toward war, and
people were calling in to cuss him out. He could've been the
start of a war himself. There was a cigarette machine in the depot.
You don't see them anymore. I remembered just two years
before being astounded that I had to go outside a depot to get
cigarettes, and now the sight of a cigarette machine was
unusual. We have finally discovered the true evil of society: tobacco. I put in some coins and down dropped a package of
Kools. I was in no hurry to get to my destination, to that job that
nobody else wanted, to that settled feeling that would just

make me want to pick up and go again, like I was now, so why not keep on this way, a new place every two or three days, stations, rain, old age, deep-fried pollock in paper envelopes with french fries and a carton of coleslaw that tastes like it has two drops of furniture wax in it?

But I have to settle. I don't have the money to be a bus-and-motel drifter, and I don't want to be one of those guys on the side of the road with a blanket roll and leathery brown skin and no teeth, completely knocked out of the loop, maybe happy, maybe free, surely independent, but knocked completely out.

And anyway, no matter how you look at it, good or bad, magic or drab, futile or purposeful, the time passes, everything passes, and the bus comes and it's dark and still raining and you get on, not too many people, and it scoots on up the road, the heater on, the wipers banging, the poor people dozing off or eating their Doritos or listening to one another's stories on this long strange trip that will one day end, that will one day no longer exist, even in memory, unless you believe George Berkeley, who said that all creation exists in the perception and memory of God, which is why the tree does not cease to exist when you turn your back and beautiful children sitting out in front of a laundromat can break your heart.

And because it was routed through Lubbock and Amarillo and Denver, the bus was soon packed with souls, packed solid with people out to do important things: deliver a water pipe, journey to a holy land, take a job in Cheyenne, visit Mom who is sick, drop off the big rig, carry the newborn into the new land. And along about evening people started to get acquainted. The sound of language overrode the rush and hum of tires on asphalt. I heard snatches of conversation:

> "I'm gonna get some money, invest in mutual funds, real estate. Don't invest in a car, man. Investment in a car is a bad idea, man."

> "First time I ever got high I was nineteen and standing in a

hole in Southeast Asia. Didn't know what country I was in.
Didn't care … "

And now each new bus I got on was so crammed I was lucky to get on at all, lucky not to have to wait four hours for the next one. In Amarillo a big black woman was angry with me for sitting next to her, but in Denver the next day, when I was running back and forth between the bus that was supposed to have my suitcase and the bus that was supposed to leave but was waiting for me to get my suitcase (which I never did get until four days later), I caught a glimpse of her and smiled and waved, and she was sweet. She had slept next to me all night, gotten to like me, even though we hadn't exchanged but a few words. "I'm sorry, ma'am," I'd said. "I know how nice it is to have two seats, but nobody is going to get two seats on this trip." So now she smiled at me as she stood looking out the tinted station window for her bus, and she was sweet because we had in a way slept together. Even though I hadn't slept.

And the bus barreled on into Kansas like a floating hospital ward: sneezing, gurgling, coughing, honking, snoring, squalling. I didn't know if Hays would work out or not, but I knew I would eventually find a place. Odessa had been wrong and Plainview had been wrong and Lubbock had been wrong and the bus didn't go to Great Bend, but the places wouldn't keep being wrong. It wasn't possible. Because things go up and things go down. That's what I ended up saying to the Mormon in Goodland after he'd rattled off his conspiracy-and-apocalypse number on me. He said his vision of conspiracy and apocalypse was grounded in the Word, but I said even God couldn't think up a plot that complicated. Sometimes it takes the wisdom of a potbellied epicurean truck driver to bring us back to reality. Things go up and things go down. It isn't much more complicated than that. The trip will be over soon enough. Don't be afraid to try the next town. You don't ever really want it to end, anyway. Halibut is good with vinegar and garlic and butter, and a little parsley on it, broiled or baked.

Advice to William Somebody

I CAN'T COUNT THE NUMBER OF TIMES I HAVE OFFICIALLY assembled the equipment to take my life: a knife, a handgun, a plastic bag, a bottle of codeine and a fifth of vodka. My motivations are never quite clear: perception of failure, futility, a sense of irremediable isolation, MTV—nothing everyone else hasn't suffered through. Yet I tend to magnify my gloomy outlook into a drive-in picture of the end of the world. I can't seem to remember that despair is a temporary state, a dark storm along the highway; that if I can just stick it out, keep the wipers going and my foot on the gas, I will make it through to the other side.

Once, while driving across the country writing suicide notes in my head for no good reason at all, I pulled off for gas in Las Vegas, New Mexico. I remember it exactly: a Phillips 66, pump number seven, $1.09 a gallon. When I went inside to pay, everyone in the store was speaking Spanish. I paid and asked the skinny kid behind the register where the coffee was. He pointed to the back. I used the restroom, then went over and got the coffee. I had decided to drive on through to Phoenix, approximately one million miles.

The store was big and new and sterile and hopeless, like the blossoming commercialism of everything. I set the large cup of coffee on the counter.

"Anything else?" asked the kid.

"Pack of Newport 100s."

He slid the cigarettes across, looking at me.

"How much?" I said.

"Two-fourteen," he said.

"For both?" I asked.

"Coffee's on me," he said.

I didn't ask him why. Maybe he was quitting after the shift. Maybe it was store policy: free coffee with every fill-up. Maybe he recognized my turmoil and understood the power of kindness from a stranger. Or maybe he represented the invisible divinity that runs through all humanity like an old F D R radio speech and only appears when you need it the most. Whatever the case, I drove on through to Phoenix without another thought of my demise.

Another time, in the other Las Vegas, where I couldn't get a job and was already five hundred in the hole and the air stank with shallow unfriendliness and mistrust, I was riding my bicycle down to the union office to see if they had found me a job. I had paid them two hundred dollars a month ago, and they still hadn't gotten me any work. (The union never did find me a job. I finally broke one of their picket lines—you know, sorry, I'm five hundred in the hole, and my rent's coming up.) That day, I was riding along in the hot June sun, secretly thinking about throwing myself in front of a truck, when I coasted by a garage right across from Bob Stupak's Vegas World (a now-defunct hotel and casino), and a black mechanic sitting on a tire in the dark, cool interior smiled at me and put up his thumb. I don't think he understood how important that single gesture was, what it meant to me.

I am ashamed to admit that I think so much about taking my life. I have no right. I am fit. I am independent. I am a member of a privileged society. A billion Third World people would give their pituitary glands to be in my position. They would probably work hard and shut up for a minute and appreciate their lives. Count me among the Querulous Generation, the thankless legion stewing alone in its own shadows; count me among the growing multitude overwhelmed by the mysterious black plague.

According to the experts, there are essentially two kinds of depression: exogenous, caused by an event outside the organism, like when your girlfriend leaves you or your best friend dies; and endogenous, which originates apparently unwarranted from some not yet understood biochemical imbalance. Both types are probably as old as consciousness. Widespread clinical chronic "endogenous" depression, however, is recent, coincidental with either music videos or the development of new antidepressant wonder drugs and the armies of manufacturers and professionals eager to recommend and administer them. Americans are a stubbornly independent lot, descendants of pirates, puritans, smugglers, and tax evaders, but we are surprisingly compliant when it comes to the offer of drugs.

Here are the profiles of four chronically depressed people I know: Gene C. (Prozac), whose wife is a tattooed cigar smoker who drives a pickup truck, has a job with the state making twice as much as him, reprimands him for even thinking she should cook dinner (though she doesn't know how to cook anyway), wants to compete with him wherever she can beat him, loathes him because "he only thinks about one thing," and then expresses frustration when he refuses to commit romantically. Gene has quit working. He sits at home all day in front of his computer and day-trades.

My eighty-six-year-old grandmother (Paxil), whose faculties have been steadily eroding for many years and whose continued longevity and precariously improving mood is almost entirely sustained by the miracle of modern medicine. She often expresses bewilderment as to why she is still alive. She cannot spell the word ocean backwards, though neither can I. According to my mother, she has recently been "completely enrolled in Kaiser," which does not mean she was made into a sandwich, although many elderly people conscripted into full-time hospital care must feel this way.

Lina (Luvox), the sixteen-year-old daughter of a friend of mine, is fifty pounds overweight and the mother of a child out of wedlock. The father is long gone. Lina's seventeen-year-old sister also has a child out of wedlock and a prescription for Luvox. Both children still live at home. Lina spends a lot of time watching television. In the evenings she works part-time at McDonald's. My friend advises me: "Have children young, so you won't be too old to raise your grandkids."

My sister (Prozac), who shares my maddening passivity, which evinces itself alternately between rage and gloom, and who feels obligated to fulfill the roll of the modern superwoman, raising four children, running a business, and driving a school bus part-time. She thinks Prozac is a panacea, and when she recommends it to me with that calm, glassy look in her eyes, I feel suddenly transported to the set of Invasion of the Body Snatchers.

Meanwhile: Life is a cellular accident. Humans are only blobs of mutated chimp chromosomes. The sum of existence is a random chemical-electromagnetic event. Death is the merciless end to a meaningless joke. Poverty is a stigma. Dependence is a psychological disorder. Love is something you find in someone else's underwear. The large rewards on earth go to the greedy, the pushy, the vicious, the base. Divorce is a happy solution to an antiquated institution. The television leaks its steady treacle of prurience, gross sentiment, concentrated doom, and pathetic idealism until we are vacant and numb, then promises relief and fulfillment through the consumption of three-day erection tablets. An impossibly high standard of living can only translate into an impossibly high level of stress. Factor in the tremendous triumphs of technology, which have given many of us not only a mistaken assumption that life should be easy and pain-free but also an illusion that we are now the captains of our fate—spiritless primate voyagers spinning through a cooling gaseous accident with nothing better to do than nibble on Pringles potato chips and read *Self* magazine until the nonsensical end—

and it is no wonder that we are the most medicated people on earth.

I have known a dozen people who have taken their lives, all of them young, none of them justified. I remember the girl in number one, who killed herself the day after I moved into a dilapidated and nearly empty apartment complex in Niagara Falls, New York. Though I'd only spoken to her once, I was horrified, struck hollow by the act. I met her father and brother that day on the stairs. They'd come to retrieve her belongings. They were haggard with grief, and reached out to me for some explanation, as if I could offer one. I grew angry with the girl and her thoughtless infliction of pain on the ones who loved her. She had thought only of herself. She had quit the game in the middle. Like a spoiled child, she had thrown all her unopened Christmas packages out into the snow.

Or I'll be leafing through a newspaper in a laundromat and see that William Somebody has died of a self-inflicted gunshot wound at the age of thirty-eight; and I'll wonder, with a little rip in my stomach: Why couldn't he make it? Why couldn't he see the absolute permanence of his mistake? Why didn't he talk to someone? Why didn't he talk to me? I could've told him: Life is sacred. Suicide is wrong. You're going to die someday anyway; why speed the inevitable?

But when my own unendurable desolation descends, I don't seem to remember my indignation at the selfishness of the girl in number one or my clear-eyed missionary advice to William Somebody. All I want is out.

The fact that I am still alive amazes me every morning. I wish I had a psychological formula, a rescue kit to hand out to my fellow melancholics. I wish I could say: This is what saved me. But each time it's something different: Kindness from a stranger. Lack of courage. Obligation to parents. Inability to write a good note. The possibility that I will have to start over again as a one-legged beggar in Tijuana or a housefly hatching out of a Dairy Queen swirl of yellow poodle doo-doo. Or I'll imagine the appearance of my corpse, its state of decomposition by the time I am found, which always reminds me of the footage of the Jonestown mass suicides and how silly these people looked, all swollen in polyester heaps and black at the fingertips—the ultimate in bad fashion.

Recently I took the worst trip of my life. It started out fairly well on a sunny, early spring day in El Paso. I got on a Greyhound bus headed north. By the time I'd reached Colorado, I was consumed in the flames of a strep infection, my back was out, and snow was falling by the foot. I got stuck in South Dakota for three days. I began to miss all the appointments I had made with friends along the way. I ended up in New York City not once, but twice in a period of twenty-four hours, the second time hobbling in a pointless, amoral fever around the labyrinth of the Port Authority Bus Terminal, talking to myself and smashing my fist into my face as hard as I could. I was trying to break teeth, draw blood, damage brains and vertebrae. People were staring at me, even the New Yorkers, who are accustomed to the insane. All the destinations looked the same to me. All the buses were the same. I stopped a woman with a clipboard whose job it was to rescue idiot travelers lost in the Port Authority.

"Can you tell me when the next bus leaves?" I said.

"Which bus?" she said.

"It doesn't matter," I said.

She seemed shocked, this woman who worked in the bowels of New York City, insane asylum of the world.

"How about LA?" I said.

She looked at her sheet. "Four o'clock," she said. "Three hours."

"What about Washington DC?"

"Half an hour," she said, squinting at me, then a glance at her clipboard. "Gate eighty-two. That's the Richmond bus."

I got on the Richmond bus, and all the way down I plotted my death as the snow flowed starlike across the glass. I wondered what everyone would think when they heard the news.

I wondered how my meager possessions would be distributed. I wondered who would care, who would laugh, who would secretly rejoice. I wondered if anyone would feel sorry for me, if anyone would miss me.

We were soon approaching DC, and I had done nothing but daydream about my end. My neck was sore, my tooth was chipped, and my cheek was swollen to the eye.

God, please, just let me die.

Then three kids boarded the bus, ball caps on sideways. They swaggered down the aisle. Each wore a new snow-white down jacket. I caught the dull nickel gleam of a gun handle in a waistband. Two of the kids dropped into the seats directly behind me. They spoke loudly for everyone's benefit.

"What'chu lookin' at?"

"Lemme see that gun."

"You ain't afraid to show it?"

"Lookit [*laughter*], I got a straight bead on the driver."

The woman next to me blanched and flattened against her seat. I felt my bladder float up into my chest cavity. Time stopped and draped itself like a braided pearl net across the aisle. One of the kids stood up. I saw the driver's eyes freeze in the mirror. I pictured the massacre photos in the next day's paper, my name misspelled, page four. Life was suddenly sweet. I prayed with a coward's softness. The snow flew past the windows.

501 Minutes to Christ

for Kim Hansen

> One might also say that an apparition is human vision corrected
> by divine love.
>
> WILLA CATHER

OUTSIDE OF A PSYCHOTIC WHO ATTACKED ME A FEW
months ago (I stuck his head into a snowbank until he promised
to leave me alone) and a middle-aged fellow who drives around
town shouting obscenities from a riding mower, there is not much
happening here in Middlebury, Vermont. It's a handsome town,
though: kindly in spirit, smart and well run, home of a fine college
with an extraordinary library. My position as cook at the Café
Chatillon down along scenic Otter Creek is more than tolerable.
So too are my living quarters: Usually I'm stuck in a room somewhere near the railroad tracks. Here I live far from the tracks in a
small, clean apartment attached to the comfy house of a middle-
class family who spend most of their time watching television.
The canned laughter fluting melancholically through the walls
has become as normal to me as the sounds of plumbing or forced
air from the vents.

I am, unfortunately, watching a lot of TV myself. The cable
is spliced in gratis from the house, and ever since I sobered up
I don't seem to get out much anymore. Granted, I could screw that
teenage girl who's been coming around, or I could have an
affair with that married woman who eyes me at the gym, but that's
all part of the old life. The old life had no meaning. I have
learned, through my many years of depraved blundering, that
men are not mere flesh, for flesh without spirit cannot move,
laugh, drink absinthe, forgive, or consider the end of time. Flesh
without spirit (see meat) simply goes bad, simply stinks.

But enough about my old life. These days I have whittled my welter of vices down to gambling (I do love the horses), two beers in the evening, and an occasional cigarette. I fancy myself an upright figure, a man of honor, a future novelist of minor distinction (even if I can't give away a story), a weight-lifting monastic hobo of whom people might say a generation or two hence, in the small likelihood I am remembered, "He was honest."

I don't recommend the writing life—at least, not the one where you move around a lot, live alone, and work odd jobs. Swing a gig where you hit the big time quick. Be a prodigy, if your agent can arrange it, and then get yourself banned in Boston. I arrived at the discipline late, at the age of twenty-nine, in part because I needed material, but mostly because I boarded a train called the Romantic Debauchery in the mistaken assumption that it would somehow get me to my destination quicker than the ones marked Hard Work and Paying Attention. Hundreds of wrong trains and many lost years later, I have learned that, despite the jovial public legends, inebriation and lucid expression are at odds with each other. If I am to write with spiritual integrity, I cannot be a drunken butterfly.

All that time I was watching those cocktails glide down my throat and powders slide up my nose, I did little in the way of maturing as a writer. I'd felt raw-nerved, out of place, and shy all my life. I found achieving worthwhile goals difficult, but talking about them was easy, especially with the help of drink and drugs, and in the company of fellow dreamers. I knew I had to quit the gliding cocktails and the sliding powders, but I did not have the courage or the know-how. Romantic Debauchery kept pulling up to the station, doors open, plenty of seats, magic confetti fluttering gaily down. At thirty-six, my pockets jammed with ripped railway tickets, I'm still scrambling to recover the lost years, still trying to "find my voice."

But now that I am reformed, a disciplined writer at last, mature at least in accumulation of years and control of appetite, I feel entitled to my modest desserts: a good night's sleep, esteem

from my neighbors, a humble career in letters, a mate, certainly—
not one of those slovenly, voracious creatures who always took
the window seat on the train, but a respectful, book-loving
brunette who owns cats, enjoys clarinet solos and avocado sandwiches, and has come, like me, the long, hard way to virtue. I'm
sure I will meet her soon.

In the meantime, after a few hours of searching for my
"voice" and a vigorous workout at the gym, I sit in front of the TV
munching on light snacks and experiencing great emotions
while watching glib characters skillfully solve personal problems
with warmth and humor on the half hour. Human intercourse
at last! I am interested in politics, sporting events, unsolved mysteries, comedy of all brands, movies, news, documentaries,
debates, interviews, biographies of serial killers and stars—anything to keep me distracted from the fact that I have once
again backed out of the human arena, afraid of getting stomped
or regressing into the old life, and I should have left Vermont
long ago.

One night, without warning, H. Ross Perot's earnest, nasal
rant about the arrogant complacency of the American people
triggers the realization of my own arrogant complacency, and self-
reproach suddenly gurgles up to my eyelids like a backed-up
sewer. I think to myself: I'm thirty-six years old and rotting in
front of a television set. The electrons that bomb that cathode-
ray tube are crumbling the cartilage of my soul, eating away my
youth and the children in my loins. I don't need to see another
riot, or plane crash, or evil twin, or clever light beer commercial,
or guy pointing a gun at me, or steroid millionaire swatting a
home run. I snap off the tube, and all those emotions that have
been sluicing into my veins, all the opinions and ideas I have
mistaken for my own, zip dizzily up into the atmosphere, and I
am suddenly a man alone on a fold-out couch in the empty
darkness of an add-on room.

Without the distraction of television, that life-support system for people with no lives, I sit for a long while, steeping in

the sudden revelation of my own stagnancy. The family next door is watching *Murphy Brown*. Why has probity not rewarded me? Why, through the exercise of conscience, am I not a measurably better human? Why, after seven years of dedicated Hard Work and Paying Attention, have I not published a single story or poem? And what will I do, I wonder, to eradicate this monstrous disgust I've amassed for myself? March back into the bar? Walk out the door and just keep walking? Commit suicide?

Instead I begin punching myself in the head. Having a palpable outlet for my hatred feels good. I'm slamming away like Marvin Hagler on Thomas Hearns in the first round of that famous three-round championship bout. I hit my nose, and blood drips onto my sweatshirt. Then it begins to pour, and I have to stop punching and cup my hand under it. I cry a bit, but it only makes the loathing worse.

After I clean myself up, I take a walk. It's a spectacularly clear spring night. Vermont is one of the prettiest places I've ever lived. I once thought I might stay here. I thought things might be different. I nod at my neighbors, pass my two old friends who always ignore me: the post office and the bookstore. There is still blood on my sweat shirt, which at least is physical proof that I am still alive. When I get home, I feel better. Self-battery has dislodged a few forgotten imperatives. I can't write anything worthwhile about America or its inhabitants if I have withdrawn from them, and no one really wants to hear another criticism of TV. It's time to throw myself back into the fire. In the morning I will give notice at work. My employer will be surprised. My employer is always surprised.

Like most people, I detest moving. Once you get started, though, it isn't so bad. You get into a rhythm when you begin throwing things away. You realize how little you really need, how much of a drain these coffee mugs and dead houseplants and Bic pens and tortilla presses are. It feels good to give away a television set or discard an embarrassing manuscript printed in dot matrix. A day or two before I leave, I usually get sick with diarrhca and worry that I'll have to cancel the trip. But I know it's just my craven way of trying to wriggle out from the duty of waking up and being alive. The diarrhea usually dries up a few hours before I leave.

There is inexpressible satisfaction in leaving my stale and cowardly life behind, in saying good-bye to the room of loneliness with its acre of rejections slips, and to the me I despise so much. Yes, I know I will see that self again soon, but for a while I will be lost, scuffling, distracted. Who knows: maybe something will happen. I will rescue children from a house fire, or a tree will fall on my head, or a famous editor will discover me, or (dare I say it) I will find the dark-haired girl.

I buy a one-way bus ticket for Louisville, Kentucky. I have always wanted to visit Churchill Downs, home of the Kentucky Derby. They just ran the derby a couple of weeks ago, so the track should be reasonably quiet, with fewer plastic mint-julep cups to wade through.

As the Greyhound leaves from Burlington, a girlish yellow-haired German woman of about fifty, wearing box spectacles and a backward white painter's cap, takes the seat next to mine. Her name is Annie, she tells me in a warm cackle of a voice, and she's going to Chicago.

I'm not much for bus conversation. It's a bit like talking to yourself. But I nod along as Annie begins to relate to me, with glittering sobriety, a story about the Death Bays of 1954, when the Indian landlords came with their Polish prostitutes and bought all the YMCAs, and for fifty thousand dollars you could sign your own death contract wherein a boy would be assigned to extract the juice from your liver, spleen, and heart, though it usually didn't work. I try not to laugh. Greyhounds have electromagnets in them that attract the disturbed and the desperate. Manic Annie talks for hours and sits with me at all the food stops, where she never eats anything, only pockets crackers and dressing packets, which she snacks upon fastidiously back on the bus while explaining the substance called "Senn" (you mean you haven't heard of it?), which melts women into creatures that resemble sheep, or her brother-in-law who nearly became a world-champion boxer but lost the European title bout because his feet suddenly began to stink.

Two states later, God bless her soul, Annie suddenly decides to change seats, though she keeps waving and whistling for me to join her in the back. I return her waves but don't get up. I've heard enough about the Polish whores who exchange their feet with yours while you sleep.

When the bus pulls into Louisville, I think for a moment Annie might follow me out the door, as she has faithfully at every stop, but when I look back she's jabbering to the man next to her about the ability of Peruvian (or Tibetan?) people to stare at you through their llamas until you are dead. And the man is in stitches, as if she were some sort of highly advanced comedian. Maybe I should have laughed instead of wasting my time being polite. Suddenly I realize that if Annie is going to Chicago, she's on the wrong bus. Oh, well, good luck, Annie. Many laughs to you. I suppose the joy of finding an appreciative audience is better any day than some feeble notion of a destination.

The letters across the depot wall in front of me read: TAXIS GAMES WOMEN—a perfect banner for my entrance into an unknown city. I've managed to strip all my possessions down to two bags: One contains my cooking tools, screwdriver, scissors, can opener, and assorted household gear. The other holds mostly clothes, an alarm clock, a Bible, and a notebook. Because bus depots represent a constant supply of temperature-controlled air, cigarettes, spare change, pinball, restrooms, snack machines, little televisions, and places to sit, they will always attract lost and marginal (and sometimes dangerous) souls in temporary need. I adjust my walk and my bearing accordingly. On the street, as it is in nature, 99 percent of all confrontations are settled or avoided by gesture, expression, and appearance, most of it false bluster. To blend in with the hustlers and their prey, I wear my bloodstained sweatshirt and crusty high-topped cooking shoes. I am unshaven. I don't smile or talk casually to people. I don't think whatever you just said was funny. I don't respond to finger crooking or "Hey, cummere for a minute." I don't give money to panhandlers. I have twelve hundred dollars cash in my left front pocket, and if you think you're getting any part of it, you are sadly mistaken.

Downtown Louisville is a slick-looking city, with green-mirrored buildings, swanky outdoor bistros, the scent of cherry blossoms, and the usual dreary sprinkle of chain outlets. I follow the business people in their suits and wonder how I will find a place to live, how I will get around. And where is that girl? She must be here somewhere, staring into her aquarium, slicing bananas into her Wheat Chex, or studying her The Ten Principal Upanishads. First things first, though. I need a map.

I duck into what appears to be a college bookstore, massive and sterile, without a single customer. "Help you, sir?" says a scholarly looking young man in a beige turtleneck.

"Map of the city?" I say, setting down my bags.

"No map of the city, sir," the young man says, adjusting his wire rims. "Maybe if you tried the gas station across the street."

"Is there a motel close by?"

He mentions the Holiday Inn, the Ramada.

"No, a cheap motel," I say. "Something with weekly rates."

"You mean the San Antonio," he says, the hint of a smirk crossing his face. "About a mile," he says, pointing down the street. "It'll be on your left."

A mile later I come upon the San Antonio, a weary-looking motel in a run-down part of town: windows cracked, letters missing on the sign, trash scattered about. Across the street an old phone booth leans in the dogwood shade. If there were another motel within a mile, I might keep walking, but I'm hungry, and my arms are tired from carrying my bags.

In the office, the clerk sits behind bulletproof glass and sips grape pop from a foam cup.

"Hello," I say.

"Hi," she replies without a glance.

A yellow sign in the corner of the glass partition reads: Competitive Hourly Rates.

"How much for a week?" I say.

"A week?" she says, as if I have just offered to buy the place.

"Yes, do you have weekly rentals?"

"Most people only stay for a few hours."

I feel flattered to get more than two words from her. "I'm traveling," I say. "I just got into town."

"A hundred and thirty-five," she says with a shrug. Throughout the entire wooden-scoop, no-touch transaction, not once does she meet my eyes.

My room is as dark as a cave, with red rubber curtains and thin, mud-brown carpet. The orange door is constructed of steel. Scrawled in pencil on the smudged walls are the names of prior guests: "Joe + Tanya = Jarrod '92" "David Ratcilff [*sic*] was here." I set my bags on the table and get a glass of water from the sink. A fiendish moaning emanates throughout the building, as if from many rooms. The German cockroaches that hang on the walls seem to be absorbing the vibration, somehow deriving nutrition from it. I turn on the television, and a greenish copulating couple swims into focus, twittering tongues entwined.

I sit down on the bed. I really don't need porno right now. I have wasted too much of my life with it already, whacking off and getting nowhere. I am far from sainthood, you understand. I spent many years indulging the flesh while the spirit languished. The bed of fertilizer from which my virtue has purportedly blossomed is sufficiently deep. I change quickly over to the news and watch a segment about gangs of black Louisville teenagers robbing whites apparently at random and then beating them to death with baseball bats. Louisville Sluggers, I imagine. A coin dealer was killed last night, says the cheerful, smooth-eyed newscaster, the third person murdered in the last month in these "wildings."

I turn off the television. Like pornography, the news is a

lurid concoction that panders to the basest emotions. I won't watch either of them, I think. I have brought French essays. I am going to study my *Daily Racing Form* and read my Bible. I need to check out the job market and the rentals. I'll find the library and continue my investigation into the mysteries of Hinduism. (Note the remarkable similarities between these second members of their trinities: Vishnu and Christ.) The girl is out there too, probably leaning out her garret window at this moment, wondering about my arrival before she returns reluctantly to her tabby cat, clarinet music, and the painting of her toenails. I'm not going to miss her this time because I'm too busy watching the narcissists preen on a twelve-inch screen or swallowing the myths offered nightly by Ted Koppel. But right now I would like to eat. And because I budget three dollars a day for my meals, I head to the Kroger across the street.

The minute I slip out my door, two hookers with extrasensitive meat thermometers, parasols tilted daintily on shoulders, whirl about and make their way toward me, their hips wagging. I hurry across the lot like a child playing Red Light, Green Light and land triumphantly on the other side of the street without speaking to them.

At Kroger I buy radishes, a box of chocolate doughnuts, four bananas, a loaf of white bread, a can of Allens chopped mixed greens, a small jar of Jif peanut butter, two York Peppermint Patties, two cans of Bush's great northern beans, one can of Goya black beans, one can of Franco-American cheese ravioli on sale, three cans of Brunswick sardines with chiles, and one can of Brunswick sardines in mustard: total, $11.29. Enough for four days.

After successfully running another gauntlet of floozies, I'm back in my motel room, my radishes floating in the sink. I have new neighbors to the east, who shout at each other.

"Retard!"

"Tramp!"

"Hillbilly!"

"Whore!"

Obviously the week with the marriage counselor was a bust.

I tie all my groceries except the canned goods into plastic sacks to keep the roaches out. As I organize my cutlery and prepare my meal, I can't resist the television. I am too curious to see what the humans are doing. For supper this late afternoon I have canned fish with chiles, a banana-and-peanut-butter sandwich, and a couple of big musky radishes while a Japanese girl massages herself with a red rubber relay baton. For dessert I eat two chocolate doughnuts and watch a moaning threesome achieve awkward release on a pool table, all still wearing their sneakers. The roaches wheel merrily around the top of the can of Franco-American cheese ravioli. The couple next door have finally stopped trading insults, and their headboard is banging. I turn on the air-conditioner fan to drown them out.

In the evening it begins to rain. I slip out for a couple of beers and a *Racing Form* and run smack into two streetwalkers cruising the front of the motel under a single gold umbrella. I step off the sidewalk to go around them.

"Excuse me," says the more attractive of the two, her lips as shiny as a cherry-frosted doughnut, "but are you staying here at this hotel?"

"Yes, ma'am, I am."

"Cummere for a minute," she says, crooking her finger at me. "I gotta ask you a question."

You know, I hate this finger crooking, this "cummere" stuff. I hold up my hand—perhaps too vigorously, for it seems to startle them both—and say, "Whatever it is, I'm not interested."

"Like, how do you know what I was going to say?" she replies indignantly, eyelids flapping, hand on hip.

"I'm not trying to be Moses, honey," I reply. "Just trying to keep my act clean."

"Shee," she replies. "Well, you in the wrong part of town for that, honey."

A few blocks down the street at Dick's Liquors, the clerk,

enclosed in his crime-resistant conservatory with the wooden transaction scoop, nods a friendly hello.

"Racing Form?" I say.

"Track is dark today and tomorrow."

"Dark two days," I say.

"Form in tomorrow about three for Wednesday."

"Which way is Churchill? I don't have a car."

"You can ride the bus for a quarter," he says. "Get you pretty close." He draws me a map.

"You play the horses?"

"Now and then."

"Nice track?"

He cocks an eyebrow. "Is there better?"

"Santa Anita?" I suggest. "Saratoga?"

"Never been to those," he says.

I buy a couple of tall Stroh's and a newspaper. That's all the money I can spend today.

That night I watch the porno for about seven hours and beat off like a teenager, my Bible and book of Malraux essays unopened on the nightstand, my newspaper, with two jobs and two rentals circled, folded in the headboard compartment. Man may not be mere meat, but flesh makes its demands. Anyway, the brown-haired girl has already turned off her radio with a sigh and gone to bed.

At midnight a party starts up next door. Perfume seeps through the vents. Ice rattles in plastic cups. Boisterous laughter fades as the porno grows louder. Water rushes through pipes in the walls. Every time a toilet flushes, my television seems to dim. The roaches float gracefully over the penciled graffiti: "ASS-HOLE." "Bridget Loves John L. Forever." The murmur of forty televisions tuned to the same channel echoes along the hallways like the groaning of chained demons in an infernal city.

Weak and ashamed from spending my seed, I sleep fitfully while guests bang in and out the steel doors for an hour or two of carnal recreation, lovers scratch the names of conquests on the walls, and roaches skitter through my sheets. I wonder why God doesn't descend to clear us all out with his staff, or break open the clouds and the dams and wash us away like rats to the sea. I wonder about Annie, who must be crossing Nova Scotia by now, maniacally slapping her thighs, every passenger on the bus roaring in appreciation. About five, I finally fall into a sound slumber and dream of a French knight wearing too much armor who goes crashing through the roof of a mansion shouting something about hors d'oeuvres.

In the morning the maid raps on the metal door with her big key ring. "Housekeeping!" she shouts. Groggily I make my way across the room in my underwear and open the door to a large pepperoni-smelling woman, who looks me up and down critically. By now I must be known by all who work here as the pitiful pud-puller who has come not just for an evening, but has thrown down money for an entire week. "You need anything," she drawls, rolling a wad of gum around her mouth. "Towels? Sheets?"

"No thanks," I say. "Come back on Friday."

She squints at me, takes out a pad, and makes a note. The next morning, and every morning after that, she will come by, rap on the door with her keys, and shout, "Housekeeping!"

ON WEDNESDAY MORNING I go to the library and sit for a while in the carpet-scented peace, reading sacred Hindu writings and wondering where all this sublime order, this fearlessness of truth, has gone. Then I take the bus to the racetrack. Hallelujah! Let's have a little fun, boys.

I've seen Churchill Downs dozens of times on television, but to view it firsthand—water fountains, banners flapping everywhere, all the decks and finery, like a grand sailing vessel built especially for bored, desperate, sexually frustrated men who've come to exercise their futility—is a privilege beyond words. The fresh air feels good. I stand by the rail and watch the horses thunder by, chips flying. Between races, I glance left and right, looking for my imaginary girlfriend.

Though I've studied and circled my *Form* carefully, and though I apply proven method and empirical principles accumulated over years of experience, I do nothing but lose at Churchill Downs for the next three days. Let's say it's the rain, the unfamiliar track, the consistently uninspiring weekday cards (little but two-year-old fillies, four-year-old maidens, and state-bred non-winners of two). Admittedly, after the track takes its 17 percent, even the most astute horse player has trouble breaking even. Though I've known many gamblers who made their living playing cards or betting football, I've never been acquainted with one who could consistently beat the horses. I have good days, which I no longer mistake for a change in fortune or proof that I've finally struck upon "the system." But I've never actually won, not over a season.

On Friday night, after losing sixteen bucks at the track, I turn in early, feeling desolate, my eyes glazed from staring at blurry images on the television screen. My brain feels physically changed, hissing and saturated with tawdry color. My Bible is a prop. The Vedas are forgotten. Malraux is dead. I can't even conjure up my nonexistent girlfriend without seeing her in pieces, a doll with detachable arms and stretch-apart lips, her stuffed cats torn to bits on the floor. I lie in bed for a long while listening to the televisions, feeling severed from humanity, wondering how the charm of solitude becomes the curse of isolation. Finally, my self-reproach rising to the Hearns-Hagler line, I lurch up out of bed, pull on my bloody sweatshirt and high-top cooking shoes, and stomp out of my groaning, scribbled-on chamber into the night.

Even angry, it isn't smart to walk in this part of town after dark. There's glass smashed on the sidewalks, a trash can overturned in the middle of the street, one house entirely covered in graffiti. A streetlight has been extinguished, shot out or shattered with a rock. Across the street a pack of snuffling mutts, noses down, offers me a collective disinterested glance before shuffling past. Antic figures in comic street poses angle toward me out of the darkness.

"You got a seg-arette?"

"You got any quarters?"

Old Spooky rides by on his ten-speed, then circles back around like a vulture. "Hey, man, what you doing in this part of town?"

In the distance a shriek rises above a wobbling siren. I hear a gate squeak, then a volley of male laughter and a sound like baseball bats clattering down picket fences. I can't help but picture Louisville Slugger trademarks embedded in my forehead and the headline in the next day's paper: "Yankee Pud-Puller Bludgeoned."

"You lost, man?"

"Hey, gimme a dollar."

I must not be far from the railroad tracks. Yet within four blocks I pass four churches. Unlike the surrounding bars, liquor stores, massage parlors, crack houses, and porno motels, all crumbling in their definition of man as pork chop, these Roman Catholic, Gothic First Methodist, Byzantine Baptist, and Greek Orthodox structures appear built to last (even if their doors are locked, their mad and destitute turned out onto the street). In the doorway of the Greek Orthodox church stands a lone sentry in a filthy robe and a gold Burger King cardboard crown, the smoky stump of a candle burning at his feet. Under his shabbily bearded and thickly lugubrious face he holds a sign that reads: 501 Minutes to Christ.

I've seen Christ twice in my life: once while stoned and all alone in a flea-ridden Mission Beach bungalow; the other time, not long ago, while praying out of the depths of my despair. On both occasions the darkness parted, and my heart was lifted with awe. In clear and sane seasons I understand that Christ is merely a refined cultural label for spirit, an archetype who will not return like Superman to save the world in its final chapter of time. But, the smell of my old life still in my nostrils, I also know that spirit (and all its archetypes and guises) is all that I will ever possess of worth.

When I return to my room, exhilarated by my reckless stroll through the ghetto and my encounter with the mystical wisdom of the insane, I smell perfume. It seems there has been a tussle on my bed. One of my bags is unzipped. I can't tell if anything has been taken. I look in the bathroom. I check behind the shower curtain and under the bed.

Many hours later keys rattle in the door. Must be the maid, I think. Then I glance at the clock: 4:20 a.m. I dredge myself from sleep, heart knocking at the top of my chest. The door creeps open across the carpet. A square of moonlight falls on the foot of the bed. A form moves toward me, then stops suddenly, strands of hair lit by the moon. My bag with the knives sits on the table across the way, open but too far to reach.

"You got the wrong room," I say, straining to keep my voice calm.

"Oh," a feminine voice replies. "I didn't know anyone was here."

"You got the wrong room, baby," I repeat, sitting up.

"You sure?" she croons.

"Get out," I say.

At the depot an hour later, two days still left on the room, I stare at a map a long while before buying a one-way ticket to Waterloo, Iowa. (Strange choice, Waterloo, symbol of a great defeat.) As I stroll about the station, I struggle with the riddle of the madman's sign. I wonder: Does 501 have some numerological significance, the way 666 does? And does the man ever update his sign? If not, there will always be 501 minutes to salvation and no one left on earth to save our wretched souls but us. For a moment I wonder if the man in the doorway was not some sort of personal apparition. I check the travel time from Louisville to Waterloo, thinking What if it's eight hours and twenty-one minutes—501 minutes—to my own salvation?

Now I'm losing my mind, seeing magic messages planted everywhere. (Travel time between the two cities is fifteen hours and fifty minutes.) No, nothing has changed. Yet I must believe in something more substantial than longevity through vitamins, or protein globules accidentally evolving into Leonardo da Vinci. Whatever I believe must have the depth and power to repel evil, insanity, loneliness, and despair. It must be built on the observation of what is good and true.

I am a shy person who lives in his head. I seek chemical and dramatic escapes from an unspectacular existence. I will likely finish my life alone in a room. Still, I can only do what I know how to do, these crude pilgrimages of moving, searching, and starting over. I am heartened by the cryptic message of the peculiar prophet in the doorway. If I am indeed spirit, eternal and indestructible, I have nothing to fear. The sun is up now, three hours to go before my bus leaves. I buy a Mr. Goodbar from the vending machine and sit down to wait.

God's Day

I USED TO PRAY A LOT. I DON'T MUCH ANYMORE. IT'S
not that I don't believe in prayer. It's just that I don't know what
to say. Asking God to bless my mother and father and all my cousins and next-door neighbors and the spotted owl over all his
other creations seems more like an Incantation of Myself than
any sort of heartfelt communication with the one who invented
avocados and time.

And there was one night when I was walking to the liquor
store in a blizzard, and it seemed I heard the babbling prayers
of all mankind, the blizzard of oh Lord, oh gimme, oh fix me, oh
help me, oh ease my busted heart and let me sleep with a
long-legged Finnish girl, but it turned out it was all my own voice,
which sounded the more pathetic in its yearning chorus.

Over the years I've developed a dubious idea of what it
might be like to be on the other end of all that begging, groveling,
and petty bargaining. Having a faint intuition of why God may
have put up the Gone Fishin' sign, I've gotten off my knees and
whittled my daily petition down to a more sensible and honest
"Thank you, God. I know I'm a fool."

Still, there is just one day in the year when I go plumb God
happy. It's a made-up day pulled randomly from the calendar,
as far away from the retail conspirators and their chocolate bun-
nies and sawed-off pine trees as I can get; a twenty-four-hour
period of gratitude, humility, and atonement, a bumbling amateur votive Mass I call God's Day.

On God's Day, from midnight to midnight, I do not eat, speak, work, smoke, read, enjoy electronic media, or accept visitors. I contemplate, and I pray. The praying is not formal; it is more conversational, something along the lines of "I hope I'm of some pleasure to you, God. I hope that I'm not getting this completely wrong. I hope I'm not an asshole. I feel terrible about that bucktoothed kid I beat up in sixth grade. And no, of course I shouldn't have slept with her, or her, or especially her." I avoid the syrupy, Goody Two Shoes approach that I suspect has put the Old Man into diabetic coma. If you're the Divine Ground, the Ultimate Reality, the Truth and the Way, no amount of sugar-coating or verbs ending in *-th* are going to mitigate the facts.

Upon the advent of my holy day, besides my fasting and tacit contemplations, I give up something important, a token sacrifice. Once, I destroyed a good story in progress. Another time I gave up watching the Michigan-Ohio State game. I always throw money away on God's Day, walk with a twenty into the darkness and leave it somewhere. Though this practice is to demonstrate a detachment from worldly things, the last few years I have begun to get a childlike satisfaction from the thought of someone needy or deserving finding the money.

Once, for example, I put a twenty in the pages of a library copy of *Charlie and the Chocolate Factory*. Several times I have dropped the money over the fence of a house in disrepair. Another time I slipped the cash into the slats of a bench in a park inhabited largely by winos.

One year I walked only a block from my motel room to the cemetery-monument company across the street. It was early November, cold wind blowing sandy snow. Around the back of the monument company was a stack of tombstones, rejects perhaps, misspelled, unpaid for, or abandoned by the contractor in a sudden change of mortal sentiment. There was one for a staff sergeant Vernon Frederick Brack, who died on my birthday in 1996. Another simply read: DWINNELL. Another large stone featured the names and birth dates of a married couple, only the wife's death date inscribed.

The heap of headstones guarded a path through the weeds that traversed the railroad tracks. And it was here where people like me—people without cars—would walk across the tracks to get to the store or to work. Unless a train derailed here, no one else but the poor would have a chance at finding my devotion. My real hope was that the Dirty Man, who walked all day, never spoke, bathed, or looked anyone in the eye, would find it. I had seen him in every part of town: walking the railroad tracks and even the old highway; on a bench by the grocery store, eating out of a discarded pizza box; or simply standing in an aisle, hands at his sides, fingers curled, staring upward, stinking and dazed, the customers flowing warily around him.

Most people did not want to admit that with an unexpected turn of fortune—a low draft number, a renegade gene, a bad marriage—they might've been the Dirty Man too. But I knew how close I'd come, how close I might yet be. I was, in a manner of speaking, going nowhere myself, getting older, still alone, and not making much progress toward my lofty goals. I had already suffered one major breakdown just two years before. I was well acquainted with the crack of Fate's cudgel, the look on his goofy sadistic face, his missing incisor and sneaky laugh. And every time I saw the Dirty Man trudging toward me, his neck collared in black skin that had once been white, shattered soul turning in his shipwrecked eyes, I felt a shiver of recognition, a vision of Christmas future.

Once I tried to give him money. It almost felt like a bribe. But too proud—or too confused—he did not acknowledge me. My recent breakdown had given me keen vision into the frail psychic condition of all sentient things, a kind of bleeding affection for anyone immersed in the cruel playground of earthly existence, even professional bass fishermen and Joyce Carol Oates. But privately I could not think of the Dirty Man in any other light than lost and gone forever, dreadful sorry, Dirty Man.

I lifted the top stone in a stack of markers and slipped in the corner of the bank note, which flapped vigorously in the breeze and met all my standards of high visibility. Satisfied, I returned home to finish my day of worship.

Though this is a hair-shirt holiday and not a turkey, gravy, and Detroit Lions one, I have never been in any danger of being swept up into ecstasy. I empty my mind of earthworms and onion rings, of gossip, news, 62 percent of sex, and up to 42 percent of daydreams, but no pictures of God have ever replaced them. I have never had a prophecy or a revelation on this day. I am never steeped in mania or visions. I have never spoken in tongues or burst out in Mahalia Jackson with full gospel choir behind me. No trace of stigmata or image of Christ's face on a cocktail napkin has ever appeared. I do not become charismatic. I just feel good for a while, cleansed, my accounts squared, at one (*see* atone), and I try to linger at the edge of this crumbling precipice before I am sucked back down into the sludgy swirl of *El Mundo*.

For my midnight breakfast I had a big dish of chicken cacciatore, two chocolate brownies, and a Coca-Cola. I sat by the window of my motel room and smoked a cigarette and watched the snow fly past the glass. From the radio I learned that I had won all three of my football bets. The money I throw away always seems to come back to me like this: "Cast your bread upon the waters," the Good Book says, "for thou shalt find it after many days," though this has nothing to do with the purpose of the day.

At 1 a.m. I went to bed, listening to the soft hiss and tick of the granular snowflakes on the window. Even though I have expended little physical energy, I never have trouble sleeping after God's Day.

The next morning it was still snowing, the same hissing, dry, crystalline flakes blowing straight-as-a-bullet sideways. I needed some groceries, so I walked the railroad tracks to the store. The twenty was still flapping in the breeze between the tombstones. Daylight had just risen. There was not yet a great deal of traffic through the frozen weeds beside the tracks, but some trailer and motel dwellers would be along shortly for the first shift at their cement-factory and tech-support jobs. I figured the bill would be gone by the time I returned from the store.

But an hour later the bill was still there. What is wrong with these people? I thought. I have been robbed twice, had bicycles and stereos stolen out from under me, there are more people who owe me money than I can count; and here I am GIVING it away, and there are no takers. I almost talked myself into reclaiming it. I could've used it. I lived on four hundred a month. It wasn't my fault that no one had picked the money up. My intentions had been good. But I knew I would feel wrong. The money was no longer mine.

The next day was sunny, still cold, and I had to go check the money. Still there, bold and flagrant as a whore waving a handkerchief at a train. My neighbor hadn't gotten his government check yet and claimed to have seventeen dollars to get him through the week. I thought of telling him, "Just go to the store, man. Walk to the store. Trust me." But that would've been too obvious, too much like a silly treasure hunt. Besides, the government was taking care of him. He'd be all right. You can't force these things. The one who needs it must find it on his own.

The bill flapped unmolested between the tombstones for three days, snow piling up all around it like sand. I couldn't understand why no one could see it. Then it occurred to me that maybe people were superstitious about fooling with tombstones, or maybe it was too easy, hidden in a place so conspicuous no one would ever find it.

On the fourth day it began to snow again, heavily, and I decided to relocate the bill. If it got buried, it might be lost forever, a fruitless sacrifice, of benefit to no one. I was missing the point of the exercise but I was stuck on the completion of my UNICEF ideal. I lifted the stone marked DWINNELL, removed the bill, shook off the snow, and stowed it away in my left pocket, the nonspending pocket.

For several days I walked around nervous and incomplete,

the soggy bill in my pocket accumulating moral weight, like something stolen or unreturned. I looked for needy children. I looked for the Dirty Man. He had always ignored me as he passed, slogging along in his cloud of eau de homelessness, but I figured I could slip the money into his jacket pocket somehow. He could buy a pizza or a package of Bugler or toss it down a sewer grate like a candy wrapper—whatever he did, it would be off my hands. My conscience would be eased. But he was nowhere to be found.

At Wal-Mart the next day a child was distressed that he could not get a toy, and I thought about secretly handing him the money. But how holy is the palliation of a spoiled child? I tried to think of worthy charities where twenty dollars didn't represent one one-hundredth of one percent of the CEO's annual salary. It's harder than you might think in small-town America to casually run across people in need. I walked around with increasing consternation and gloom.

My sacred day was stretching out into an eternity of worldly snags. I was ready to throw the money into the gutter or tear it up like confetti or leave it blowing across the snowy grounds of the graveyard, when I passed the Immaculate Heart of Mary Church. Although I was aware there had been an evil pope in the fourteenth century, and Catholic ritualism often rivaled many American sporting events, I also knew that Catholic charities did good work. Every person I'd ever met who'd gone to a parochial school for any length of time had a better education than I had, and deeply inculcated guilt and a well-illustrated idea of hell usually make for more interesting and intelligent company than the average Joe with a healthy sex life and oodles of self-esteem.

Two older women were entering the church. I thought they must be very religious to be attending services on a weekday evening.

"Excuse me, ma'am," I said to the one bringing up the rear. She was a bent, small woman of perhaps seventy-five years. "Are you a member of this church?"

She looked up at me, her eyes so peaceful and blue I knew I had come to the right place. "Yes, I am," she said.

I handed her the twenty. "Could you give this to the church? Put it in the collection plate or something."

She accepted the money without question or even curiosity, as if this were an everyday occurrence, as if she had been expecting me.

"I'll put it in the box by the Virgin Mother," she said.

"Thank you," I said.

She said thank you too, so radiant with peace and self-assurance I almost wanted to follow her in, become a Catholic too, except for that evil pope in the fourteenth century.

I was ready to feel good now, to go home and drink a glass of sacramental wine. But then here came the Dirty Man, plodding along in his mindless fugue, dressed in grimy khakis and tan leather jacket and split black brogues, the stump of a hand-rolled Bugler burning in his fingers. I slowed my pace and braced my heart. Soot-speckled snow was packed in the gutters. The sun was almost down, the sky a hazy golden pink. The rough smell of cattle in the air mingled with the stench of the Dirty Man. As he passed, he raised his head and wrung from his leather face a smile that seemed troubled and shy. "Hello," he said.

I was shaken. "Hello," I returned.

I had more to say—"What's your name?" perhaps, and, "Can I buy you a pizza?"—but he was gone.

Who knows what form will spin next from this glittering snarl of dragons and clowns we call our soul? Perhaps this time next year I will be the one walking the tracks or lifting a slice of trash-can pizza to my insane lips, while he, on good meds and cleaned up in a pressed, striped shirt, casts about for a clever way to dispose of a twenty-dollar bill. In the meantime, feeling once more the pull of the earth, I promised myself two glasses of wine that night in my warm little room, maybe even three, and then I waved to no one in particular and headed out, muttering at the sky: "Thank you, God. I know I'm a fool."

Realism

Speak the truth with one foot in the stirrup.
ARAB PROVERB

FOR ABOUT TEN MONTHS I WORKED AT A RADIO-ANTENNA
factory in the tiny town of Hays, Kansas. The factory workforce
was comprised mainly of the inexperienced, the handicapped,
the socially discarded, the desperate, the just-out-of-jail, and
the fallen-to-the-bottom-of-the-ladder, with a handful of cheerful, non-English-speaking Mexicans thrown in. The starting
wage was fifteen cents above the minimum. The work was mono-
tonous but undemanding. The average employee lasted probably
two weeks.

I was recovering from a nervous breakdown, or whatever
you call it when you realize you are a complete failure and you
fall down crying and can't get back up again. The compactness
and simplicity of my room at the Sunset Motel reassured me.
I had my ritual. I was not interested in traveling. (I had lived on
the road, off and on, for years.) Nor was I interested in being
worldly, or in finding the answers to deep questions. I felt lucky to
still have my independence and my health. I read the Bible every
night because it gave me comfort and because all the writers
I admired read the Bible, and I wanted to be a successful writer.

I was reasonably content at the radio-antenna factory.
I appreciated the sameness of the days, the lightness of the tasks,
the proximity to the motel. (I had no car). And I had weekends off to write. I worked in the welding department, where we
sanded, machined, and "straked"—wrapped wire braids
around— mast antennas for Ford, GM, and Chrysler. I watched

other employees come and go. Our department received at least one fresh applicant a week. Sometimes the new guy didn't even finish a shift. The factory was gritty and loud. The owner treated us like children, touring the floor daily to point out our short-comings, or else his voice came over the PA to inform us that we were not meeting our quota, or that a holiday would have to be suspended due to a deficit in production. Once, he announced, without irony, that we would no longer be able to listen to our radios. Whenever a healthy adult male reported for his first day of work, I wondered what kind of trouble he was running from. Four of the healthy adult males on our line had weekly appointments with parole officers.

When Russ from Topeka showed up, I estimated he would last two days. He had the face of a heavily tranquilized mule, black plastic-framed glasses (which kept sliding down his nose), a neatly trimmed mustache, and a slope-shouldered stance, palms turned back. Mike the foreman let him weld for a couple of hours, saw that he had no aptitude, and put him on the rod machine next to mine.

I showed Russ how the machine worked: place ball tip on end of rod, slot base plug into chuck, drop rod between hydraulic clamps, press buttons, whoosh-thump: machined car antenna. I explained that he would eventually be expected to produce four hundred antennas per hour. (Five hundred was the official quota, but only a showoff could keep up that pace.)

"Piece of cake," Russ said, and he took his seat.

"What brought you to Hays all the way from Topeka?" I asked.

"Got mangled in a bicycle wreck," he replied. "Four hundred stitches. Mashed up my head pretty good." He grinned.

I didn't know what a bicycle accident had to do with moving to Hays, but I didn't pursue it. Clearly something was wrong with him. He had the thick, slurred speech of the mildly brain damaged. A vague jigsaw pattern of scars covered his face, as if he'd recently undergone dramatic but unsuccessful plastic surgery. He flashed a slightly crooked, incongruent, but pleasant smile. He said he was thirty-two years old. As he assembled antennas, his gaze wandered around the factory. The three of us who worked the rod machines had trouble conversing because of the mandatory earplugs and the endless whoosh-thump (four hundred an hour, times three) of our machines, but Russ lifted his voice over the racket to narrate a barely coherent account of how he and his cousins, whom he was living with, had video-taped their own version of *Home Improvement* in their basement the night before. "It was funnier than hell," he shouted, taking his hands off the machine and sticking his finger in his nose, apparently to illustrate one of the funnier parts.

Kathy, the spot welder to my left, turned from her magnifying glass and gave me a look that said: Where did this goofball come from? Because there was already a Russ on our line, the new Russ instantly became "Home Improvement." Home Improvement produced about twenty-five antennas in his first hour, half of them without ball tips.

"This is pretty easy," he said.

"Try to put ball tips on the ends," I said. "Some people are picky about that kind of thing."

He smiled good-naturedly and began to list and summarize the plots of all the science-fiction videos he'd watched over the past week with his cousins. "I like to escape," he explained. "I have enough realism in my life."

Russ and I had lunch together at a picnic table. It seemed I always bonded with the new guy, perhaps because after more than sixty jobs and at least a hundred moves—all in pursuit of the writing dream—I knew all too well what it was like to be the new guy. For lunch, Russ had brought a half pound of baby carrots (one of his cousins ate a pound a day, he told me), an apple, and a cola. I learned that his driver's license had been revoked for multiple drunk-driving violations. He alluded to a wild past and a romantic life of drifting from town to town. As he answered my questions, I got the impression he would say whatever he thought might impress his listener.

"I'm trying to get over being callous and cold," he said, lifting his scar-paneled face to mine, as if he were James Dean enduring the burden of misunderstood greatness. "That's what they call me."

"Why do they call you that?"

He shrugged and popped another baby carrot into his mouth. "I used to drink three or four cases of beer a day."

"That's about a can every ten minutes," I observed.

"I had help," he said. "My friends would come over."

"It's good to have friends."

He nodded, the slightest flicker of doubt (fear?) in his eyes. "My ex-wife was a stripper," he said. Then he added, with moral sobriety: "She quit dancing six months after we got married, but she's still suffering the effects."

"You got kids?" I said.

"Two," he answered, "and two from her previous marriage."

"How old?"

"Six and eight. I don't remember how old hers are."

"What are you doing working for minimum wage if you have two children to support?"

"It's an easy job to get," he said.

"How do you make ends meet?"

"I've got another job. I'm painting my cousins' house. I'm a painter by trade."

The next day at lunch Russ bought a bag of Bugles and a Pepsi from the snack machine. All morning, while he'd worked, he had daydreamed aloud about getting his driver's license back. His life seemed to revolve around this event, which was more than a year away. Once he got his license back, he would get a car, and probably a trailer, too; he planned to be mobile for the next two years. Also, he thought he might buy a house—a big place, two bedrooms at least, so his kids could stay with him. A minute later he was going to rent a small apartment so he could save some money. I wondered if his short-term memory had suffered the most damage.

"It won't be long," he said, "before the court puts a 55 percent child-support garnishment on my paycheck."

"Seems like it would be cheaper just to stay married."

"Too late," he said. "Can I borrow a cigarette?" He leaned back against the picnic table, puffed on his cigarette, and began to muse on romance. "Got a girl coming to see me this weekend from Topeka. Think I just might buy me a Harley-Davidson."

The next day Russ announced proudly: "I haven't had a drink for two years, nineteen days."

"Congratulations," I said.

"God is the answer," he said earnestly.

Half an hour later, Russ asked if I wanted to go out after work for a beer.

"Can't," I said. "Have to work."

"On what?"

"I write."

"Oh? What kind of stuff?"

"True life," I said.

"I like realism," he said. "Will you write a book for me? I'll pay you."

"A book on what?"

"My testimony." He gave me his quick-flash smile. "But I'm afraid you'd see who I was and say, 'Whoa.'"

"The more *whoa*s, the better the book," I said.

"I like to live on the edge," Russ said.

Russ couldn't remember anyone's name except mine and the foreman's. He slunk around in his James Dean fog, parroting the tired lines of the day. ("Been there, done that.") His coworkers weren't even remotely interested. He never machined more than 150 rods an hour. Often he was not putting on ball tips. "They can't expect speed and quality," he said indignantly.

After two weeks, Russ was transferred to a less-demanding department, the mercury-lamp line. At lunch, in between clichés, he told me he didn't think he would be able to stay on the new line. "There's too much jumping around," he said. "I need to relax while I work. Like on the rod machine."

Though everyone else instinctively wrote Russ off, I continued to give him the benefit of the doubt. I had known a few other head-injury cases. In every instance, the before and after were two different people. A self had to be rebuilt from scraps, sometimes from smoke and mist. I wondered: What if you started with the wrong part? What if the very foundation of your existence was a lie? How would you ever know? Russ, I suspected, had not always been a drifting, sleazy cliché monger. The real Russ was down there somewhere, like a man trapped in a collapsed mine. I thought I could see him struggling to get out while the crazed, bogus Russ prattled heedlessly on.

I had been obliterated by fate myself. I was forty-two, and all I had to show for my years of privation, hard work, and anonymity, were more privation, hard work, and anonymity. I wanted to write something true. I had ridden my Big White Steed of Truth into the craven world and been knocked face-first into the mud. After wandering around sobbing and rearranging the letters s-u-i-c-i-d-e for a year and a half, I'd landed in that motel room, where I sat with the curtains closed, underlining passages in the Bible, two rejection slips waiting for me in my post-office box. The writing dream was dust. Mystery had supplanted truth as my religion.

I once read an interview with Kurt Vonnegut in which he talked of his disenchantment with scientific truth because "we dropped [it] on Hiroshima." Vonnegut's metaphor is apt: The truth is no flickering Hawaiian lantern. It is searing white light. It scorches roaches and saints alike. It can flash a liar to cinders and in the same stroke smoke the poor bozo next to him who all the while thought that God was on his side.

Having no real acquaintance with reality, Russ did not fear the Truth. He talked about God, church, and family, misquoting the Bible and fumbling Republican TV sound bites. Undaunted by any question, he possessed that special brand of liquid ignorance

that covered every subject like a high-tech fertilizer. He edu-
cated our coworker Pock—a Buddhist welder from Thailand—
about Thai culture. (Russ had once had a Thai girlfriend.) He
told a group of us how someone had once tried to rob him with a
9mm, but Russ had whirled on the mugger, grabbed the gun,
and shot him in the leg. (He later pawned the gun for fifty dollars.)
He was embarrassing to listen to. Was it possible that he
thought everyone was as insincere and ignorant as he? I didn't
know what, if anything, about him was true.

One day Russ decided it was time to move out of his cousins' house. (I suspected he was being kicked out.) I told him
there was a vacancy at the residential motel where I lived. He followed me over after work to have a look. He was dressed in an
athletic jersey with a zero on the back and a crisp baseball cap
that read: "Walk by FAITH, 2 Corinthians 5:7."

The Sunset Motel was down by the railroad tracks and had
a turnover rate similar to that of the radio-antenna factory.

"Pretty nice," Russ said, standing in the doorway of my
room. Like all the rooms, it had changed little since the Great Re-
decoration of 1958: same hamster-cage air conditioner, smoke-
tinged chenille curtains, Second Empire desk and dresser,
cracked vanity mirror, billiard-green carpeting, black-and-white
Zenith TV, and collapsed, love-stained mattress. In the sun-
light, I could see all the scars on Russ's face, the odd shape of his
skull, the looseness in his eyes and jaw. Something had really
walloped him. If I'd been hit like that, I thought, I'd probably be
a blithering idiot too.

"How much?" he said.

"This one's two hundred, but it has a sink and a range. The
sleeper has no kitchen, and it's smaller."

"That's cool. I won't be in much anyway."

"Linda, the manager, isn't here now," I said, "but she should
be home soon."

He nodded. "You have a computer."

"Yes."

"Is that what you write on?"

"That's right."

"When I get my license back ... "

Russ moved into room eighteen, a sleeper with a microwave and fridge, $185 a month. He furnished it with stacks of milk crates, a television, and a VCR.

I stopped by that afternoon to see how he was getting along. He was reclined on the bed, legs crossed.

"How do you like it?" I asked.

He clasped his hands behind his head and gave a satisfied sigh. "I'm just going to hang out and save my money."

I thought, A 55 percent child-support garnishment at five dollars an hour, and you'll be able to save about forty dollars a month.

Though he worked in a different department now, Russ continued to sit with me at lunch. Other times of the day I saw him standing off by himself, a lost figure, waiting for his next department transfer. "Hey, Home Improvement," everyone greeted him. He sneered, pulling back further into his James Dean fog. Whenever he saw me, he brightened and called out my name, as if he were seven years old and I had just turned the corner in my ice-cream truck. Try it, Russ, I wanted to say to him. Tell the truth just once. See how it feels. Witness the benefits, like job security and people who don't despise you. What have you got to lose?

We walked to and from work together. One day, crossing the railroad tracks, he pointed suddenly at the ground and said, "Those plants are marijuana."

As we negotiated the patches of wild "marijuana," I considered the irony of our unlikely alliance: dark charlatan and wounded cynic. We had arrived here by different courses, but to the naked eye we were indistinguishable: drifting factory workers crossing the tracks to their single rooms.

"I need me a job that makes more money," Russ said miserably.

"Now there's an idea."

The next morning he knocked on my door at six, obviously upset. "My son's been in a bicycle accident. I have to get back to Topeka. Can you tell them at work I won't be back for a few days?"

"Of course," I said. "How are you going to get to Topeka?"

"My uncle is going to give me a ride."

"Go," I said.

When he returned a week later, I asked him about his son.

"He's fine," he said. "Just a concussion. I had a long talk with him about bicycle safety."

Just the man to give it, I thought.

"I hate him," said Linda, the motel manager, who came to my room for coffee once in a while. Linda was constantly vexed by tenants: drunks who forgot their keys at two in the morning, late-night banjo players, secret ferret owners, non-rent-payers, people who dismantled engines in their rooms or tried to have indoor barbecues. But Russ had her more worked up than I'd ever seen her.

"He came over to use the phone the other day," she said. "He said he had a local call to make. I got the bill yesterday, and he'd made three long-distance calls." She held up three fingers. "He also borrowed my car. He drove it all the way to Topeka. Do you know he doesn't have a license?"

"Why did you give him your car?"

"He said his son had a bicycle accident. I talked to his wife. His son didn't have any bicycle accident."

"How did you get ahold of his wife?" I asked.

"Her number was on my phone bill." She took a sip of coffee and lit a Salem. "I won't repeat what she said about him."

"They're divorced," I said.

"According to her, they're still married." Her hands were trembling. "He's the biggest liar I've ever met."

"And not a very good one, at that."

"If it's one thing I can't stand," she said, "it's a liar."

"I've got me a check for eighteen thousand dollars," Russ told me a few days later at lunch.

I nodded but said nothing. Send a few bucks home to Topeka when you get a chance, I thought. People are counting on you.

At 3:30 that afternoon, as we headed out the factory doors, he was still talking about the check, which was now down to five thousand dollars. Before we had turned the first corner, he said, "You should've seen this guy at work today. I really turned his head. 'How much you want for that car?' I said. 'Five thousand,' he said. 'I'll give you twenty-five hundred cash for it right now,' I said. 'Got me a check for three thousand dollars.'"

Russ had been transferred to soldering, his third department. He was having trouble with quality control and wasn't getting along with his fellow employees. He couldn't accept the idea that people did not like him because he was lazy and constantly lied. In the mercury-lamp department, he said, he had tried to "kid around with the kids," and they'd turned on him. Now he was happy to be with "adults, like myself."

"I'm just going to sit back and play it cool," he said.

When he was transferred out of soldering, Russ decided it was time to find a better job. He knocked on my motel-room door. "I need to print my résumé," he said.

"Bring it by after seven," I said.

That evening he handed me three ragged notebook pages scrawled on with pencil. Except for a security-guard position that he'd floated in and out of for two years, he'd never kept a job longer than six months. At Frito-Lay, he was "let go for reasons beyond my control."

"Frito-Lay must have been a pretty good job," I said.

"Yeah," he said. "They give you free Doritos. I got tired of Doritos, though."

"You've got these big employment gaps," I said. "Employers generally don't like that."

"Oh, I drifted around from state to state for a few years," he said.

Every one of the jobs listed, since he was seventeen, had been in Topeka.

"I'm gonna get me a computer here pretty soon," Russ said.

"What are you going to do with it?"

"Learn how to use it."

It took me an hour and a half to correct his spelling, fill in the gaps, and get the dates to agree. Judging by his sad little work history, he had not been changed in any essential way by the head injury. I had wanted a glimpse of the real Russ, and there he'd been all along, sitting on my bed, waiting for me to finish his résumé.

The next morning was Saturday. Russ came over early, while I was writing, and shouted my name as he knocked on the door. He was holding his résumé again. "I need you to rewrite it for me," he said. "There's a couple more things I thought of."

"I'm working, Russ."

He craned his head to peer into the room. "I have to have it by tomorrow," he said. "I'll be glad to compensate you," he added, sensing my disapproval. "I'll take you miniature golfing."

"The library is open," I said. "They have public computers."

"I don't know how to use them."

"Well, it's time you learned."

On Monday morning, I made sure Russ left before I did. Even so, I caught up with him just across the tracks. He had taken a wrong turn and was lost.

"Kind of foggy this morning," he said.

I pointed in the direction of the factory, and we began to walk.

"Sorry about the résumé," he said. "I didn't mean to inconvenience you."

"Did you go to the library to finish it?"

"No, my aunt helped me," he said. "She has a typewriter."

As we walked, Russ related to me his dream of working for Allied Concrete, which we passed on our way to and from the factory every day. He explained how the better-paying companies were more selective. (Really?) He thought he might be able to get on with Allied because he'd driven a Mack truck before. (I don't recall that on your résumé.) The interviewer, he said, had told him to keep sticking his head in the door.

I was surprised when Russ got a job, not at Allied, but with another firm on the outskirts of town, some kind of maintenance position that paid $8.90 an hour, or so he claimed. "I'm making twice as much as you now," he crowed. "The big bucks!"

I smiled and shrugged and wondered how many times he'd been knocked down. Maybe there had never been a bicycle wreck, only people knocking him down.

Though his license was still suspended, Russ bought a car for two hundred dollars from one of the more desperate tenants and drove it, still registered under the seller's name, to and from work. I didn't see him much after that. He claimed to be working seven days a week, plus overtime, pulling down three grand a month. Once, however, he came over to my room to borrow a dollar.

The next time I talked to Russ, he told me angrily that he'd been demoted. They'd cut his salary and switched him to the graveyard shift. He said he was thinking about quitting.

Not long after, Linda told me that Russ had stopped paying the rent. He'd wait for her light to go off before sneaking into his room at night. In the morning he would leave before she got up. She didn't think he was working anymore. By the end of the month, she'd evicted him. The last time I saw him he was walking out of a bar on Vine.

Call me naïve if you like, but I never regretted my kindness to Russ. I don't believe kindness can ever be wasted.

"I've lived on the edge most of my life," Russ told me. "I enjoy the rush. Most people wouldn't understand."

No, Russ, I understand. Realism is brutal, and the truth is a killer that none of us want to face.

Blessed Meadows
for Minor Poets

I find that most people know what a story is until they sit down
to write one.

FLANNERY O'CONNOR

AT TWO O'CLOCK IN THE AFTERNOON ON MARCH 18, 1998,
while typing up a story on a snowy gray day in room number 8
of the Sunset Motel, Hays, Kansas, I heard the crackle of tires in
fresh snow out front. I had just quit the radio-antenna factory a
month before, having saved enough to write for two more months
before I would have to go back. Though I was forty-two and had
given up woman, dog, and comfy job for this writing "career," my
life was not taking any significant shape. If I'd been earmarked
for success it should've happened long ago.

Then someone knocked on my door. It was the FedEx man,
standing in the snow. I didn't know who would be sending
me anything FedEx. I signed for the package, thanked him, and
closed the door. The letter inside the cardboard envelope read:
"It is my pleasure to inform you that Garrison Keillor, guest editor
of the 1998 edition of the *Best American Short Stories*, and I have
chosen your story 'The Blue Devils of Blue River Avenue,' originally published in the *Sun*, for inclusion in this year's volume."

I thought it must be a joke, though I knew no one who
could fabricate such a convincing letter. I had never much liked
these *Best American Short Stories* (BASS), but now, as I reflected
on them, I decided they were pretty good after all. I realized
this was a huge boost to my "career." I wondered why they had
picked this particular story. It hadn't been nominated for anything. I'd never gotten one letter on the thing. At the same time
I understood that much of what happens in the literary world is

a lottery, and I had been plugging away for a while, so maybe it was time for my head to bob up above the sea of drowning writer heads, if only for a few minutes.

I went next door and showed the letter to Chick, my neighbor, who was striving to be a painter and was probably the only one in this residential motel—perhaps in all my circle of working-class acquaintances—who could appreciate what had happened. Chick didn't know what a BASS was, but he recognized the name of the guest editor, Garrison Keillor, and he let out a crow. Chick liked Guinness, so I bought a sixer and we raised a few creamy black draughts to the snowy gray sky in honor of the lottery that consistently rewards artists who do not deserve to win, who are just there, but keeps all us self-proclaimed artists going and fills us with hope. A reward for mere persistence is not such a bad idea.

My parents were thrilled when they heard the news. They had been reading my painful, difficult stories and patiently putting up with my infinitely slow growth, perpetual penniless-ness, and occasional collapses for years. Now they had some-thing to tell the neighbors and relatives, who secretly thought I was a bum and would secretly continue to do so since they had never heard of BASS, and I wasn't rich yet or on television.

The BASS award paid five hundred dollars—which meant five more weeks away from the factory—plus an additional hundred if my story were deemed fit for an audiotape narrated by Mr. Keillor himself. It was! Imagine that: six hundred dollars for a story that took me only six years to write. If you're dreaming of the big bucks, fiction writing is definitely the field for you. You might also consider milk delivery, door-to-door encyclope-dia sales, or shoeing cart oxen.

I walked around in the clouds for a whole day, telling any-one who would listen about my big jackpot. But then it was time to get back to work. I'd had my little fling with fortune, and if I wanted another, I'd have to sit down and write hard for ten more years, drop as many tickets into the raffle barrel as possible.

More importantly, I hoped to sell something to buy one or two more months away from the factory.

But then something even stranger happened: The hallowed American publishing house Burns and Sons (not its real name) asked to see more of my work. Was I under contract? they wanted to know. Did I have an agent? Did I have a novel they could look at? A collection of stories? I told them I had a dozen novels in various states of disrepair, but I had many completed, published stories. They said please send the stories. I couldn't take them seriously. I thought of stories only as exercises for the novel I would complete one day. No one reads stories. Name me the last collection of stories on the best-seller list. Stop a hundred people on the street and see if one can give you the name of a contemporary short story writer besides Stephen King. If you're in the mood to lose a quick investment avoid commodities and Ponzi schemes and start a magazine that publishes short stories. I had been knocking myself out for ten years and couldn't even get an agent, and now the largest publisher in the world was blithely asking me to send them a bunch of stories.

Things got even weirder when B&S decided they would publish the stories. I signed a five-year contract for five thousand up front and five thousand upon delivery of manuscript. And since the manuscript was already complete (I thought) I was suddenly two years away from ever having to return to manual labor. My future rolled out to the horizon with red carpets, smoking jackets, and trumpet music: the story collection would sell, B&S would take all twelve of my novels as I spun them into dazzling form, I would tour the country, do Oprah two or three times (Oh, God, Poe you're wonderful) and mumble at various university podiums for ten thousand a pop about character development and the need for world peace.

I was assigned to an editor. I liked her at first. Even if when you rearrange her name it spelled Idiot P. Hitler! We'll call her Virginia. She seemed competent and energetic. She seemed to have a good sense of humor. She seemed overworked. She thought my stories were "terrific." Even if she was young (she imagined that children in 1965 might spend a rainy day inside playing video games), she had been hired by one of the savviest, burliest, most profitable publishing outfits on the planet, so she had to be good. I didn't know where she came from or who or what she had edited before. All I knew was that she was young and an assistant to another editor. Should a beggar demand to see the chef? I was too grateful to be out of the rain while my old battalion, the 107th Dreamer Division, huddled in their soggy coats and pressed their noses longingly against the glass.

I was pretty old for my first book—according to our publishing schedule, I would almost be forty-four by the time it appeared—and I knew that B&S had signed me as a long-shot prospect. Getting me under contract was like optioning movie rights, a cheap freeze on the competition in case I did something interesting (or profitable). My first book would have a limited print run, ten thousand, and it would be in paperback. No big promotional plans were in the works. I understood that this might be only a peep at the big time. I was like a character from the movie *They Were Expendable*, and the editor was studying my hazy frames with a pair of scissors in his right hand.

Still I was stubborn. No way in my power would I go back to the minors and hit pop fouls in front of those small crowds again. I'd had day jobs for twenty-five years now. I'd paid my dues. So when Virginia sent me the B&S style manual, *A Guide for Authors*, and a personal three-page letter on how to write ("I know this is a lot to absorb"), I took it in stride. Certainly I had room to grow. I was no Thomas Wolfe. I didn't even have a college degree. Virginia gave me the impression that out of the fifteen stories I'd sent her, all of them published, we were just about there.

But Virginia did not like travel stories, or drinking stories, or stories that sounded like nonfiction. She didn't think it credible or prudent that my characters quit jobs without giving notice (the way I did), that many were obsessed with suicide (the way I was), that romance was a guaranteed bust (me again).

She liked childhood stories, like "The Blue Devils of Blue River Avenue," the BASS winner. This cut the number of potential candidates from fifteen to four and made me look like that guy who wrote Mr. Popper's Penguins. But who was I to argue? I was free from the factory. I had almost seven grand in the bank and a book coming out and unlimited potential. You take a little, you give a little. There is no success without compromise. I had a bundle of material and experience. I was endlessly adaptable. Certainly I would be able to come up with a few more stories.

Virginia and I talked on the phone at first, collect calls I made from the Hays, Kansas, public library. I felt as if I were talking with someone whose feet had never touched the ground, who had worked part-time at McDonald's for one summer before obtaining her MFA from Cornell University and then immediately moved into plush chambers littered with Diet Coke cans in a tall building that smelled brightly of carpet where people on their coffee breaks glowed about John Updike. I mumbled and hawed. She was cordial, complimentary, and encouraging. I discovered that she was assigned to "new" and "young" writers, of which I was neither. A little fold rose in the landscape between us and took the shape of a mountain. Eventually we returned to the remote safety of our personal computers.

As the stories went back and forth from Kansas to New York, a pattern emerged: she didn't generally like my endings, the beginnings were not much better, and frequently the middles were not right either. She was obsessed with "character motivation," "setting scenes," and thought that the secret to success was "draft after draft." I believed in rewriting too, though I'd learned that if you didn't have anything in the first place, if you were not addressing the main problems, if your characters were not alive, if the purpose of the story was not clear (especially to the person or people writing it), if you kept turning left down dark alleys instead of right toward the lighted avenues, then no amount of rewriting would alter the fact that you were finger painting in a heap of llama droppings.

Virginia, however, "new and young" herself, just off four straight years as president of the Cornell pep club, and eager to show her B&S superiors that she could whip this droll drifter into shape, was tireless. Draft after draft we went, like an arranged-marriage couple on a forced honeymoon varnishing stove-in boats washed up along the Bay of Fundy. A perfectionist, driven to achieve at all costs, she was tyrannically opposed to the word something. Neither would she permit the word spinster. My dialogue, without much exception, was "flat." I used the word yellow too much. Free from manual labor with nowhere special to go, I began to write ten, sometimes twelve hours a day. My first book, unless I wanted to die on the vine, had to be brilliant.

After six months or so of energetic heaving and arduous grinning and slapping about of lacquer brushes, Virginia and I had come up with nothing. I should say less than nothing because the stories that had survived the first cut (even the BASS winner) had been changed to the point that I was having trouble recognizing them.

To give her credit, maddeningly ingenuous though she was, Virginia was ever positive, especially about new stories I'd create, since the old ones were in a shambles, like heaps of broken toasters with so many burnt crumbs among the twisted elements. But all the new stories went through the same hopper, and before long I lived in a fiendishly disheveled world of suspended and abandoned stories, stacked in drifts like shifting sand dunes across my motel-room floor. I barely had a path to the front door. My neighbor, Chick, who came by once a week to hoist a few with me on our only nights of society, worried that I might be lost and never recovered, like some poorly outfitted spelunker.

When another story fell from the ranks, leaving three, I confided to Virginia that I didn't think I could do this anymore. I've never written under pressure, I explained. I've never willed a story to exist. Because I'm slow and haven't found the philosopher's stone yet, I have to write ten stories to get one good one. They come from the Land of Mystery on their own. Often, like the BASS winner, they take years to develop, moving from novel to story to poem to essay and back again. And then, eventually, if I'm lucky, I have an accident: type the wrong word, or marry two disparate entities, or stumble across a solution in a newspaper article about a bipolar shoplifter in Mobile, Alabama. I'd like to write in a more organized, predictable way, but I gave up on science fiction long ago. I know at Cornell they teach you that S (Story) = 123, but it isn't true, not a real S anyway, not an S that doesn't have an H right after it, followed by a quick IT.

It was not in Virginia's job description, her training, or her nature to be straightforward, and, to be fair, I think she didn't really know what to do either. Who wants to be lowered down here in the darkness with just mystery and me? But I understood she was obliged to keep up my spirits. Even in my moments of darkest doubt, Virginia never lost heart, though now and then she had to go to Rome on a two-week vacation.

I had never in my life felt creatively dead. I had never suffered from "writer's block." I don't believe in writer's block anymore than I believe in speaker's block. If you have something to say then say it. If you have nothing to say, then you shouldn't be writing, or speaking, in the first place. If your hand is cramped then use the other one. If you can't write a novel, then "writer's block" is going to save you a lot of time and trouble. Writer's block is a blessing to us all, but because there are eight hundred thousand new books published every year, and millions of eager writers eager to trample the front-runners, obviously there is not enough of it to go around.

And neither was my problem "artistic integrity." I was accustomed to aggressive editing. Talk with any writer who has dealt with the *Sun*, and you'll hear a legendary tale of leviathan transformation. The editorial staff at the *Sun* runs all submissions through giant paper shredders, turns the mounds over to caged marmosets on amphetamines with ice hammers, bellows Sufi war chants long into the moonlit night, and then begins the almost supernatural process of hand-dipping each shred of paper into Japanese squid ink before returning the manuscript, miraculously restored, to its sender. But I found this process relaxing compared to working with Virginia, primarily because the editors of the *Sun*, even though it might take a year to get a story to their specs, know what they're doing. True, I was often puzzled and even disgruntled at the final version, but the point is we did produce, we did publish. I was paid, and the work was often improved and even salvaged. I received adoring letters, money, and photographs from admirers. Many of the stories were nominated for prizes; two won major prizes; several were short-listed in anthologies. Many were reprinted in other publications. In other words, the relationship was beneficial.

So why at my last chance of entering Blessed Meadows for Minor Poets, did Virginia stand like an evil troll at the gates? I began to wonder if I'd sold out. Were the gods punishing me? Was it possible that I needed to remain poor to keep my honor? Could Virginia, who represented most of what I thought was wrong with the scholastic approach to writing, be some sort of divinely planted obstacle to test my faith? And if I passed the test (i.e., forfeited the contract) were even greater rewards waiting for me beyond? I only had one hard, fast rule at the time: if you get between me and the writing, out you go. But who would've ever dreamed that an editor at a giant publishing house, the wizard I had worked so hard to see, would be the one to get in the way?

As the stories were shipped back and forth, our cordiality cooled. My jokes to relieve growing tension seemed inept and crude. For lethargic hours every night I studied her penciled changes and rewrites, which seemed to yearn for grad school where she always got an A and then threw the project away. I had ceased to produce anything on my own. I felt something like Virginia's puppet. Oops, I used the word something. Day after day I stared into my amber screen and wondered why hard work didn't pay off. What had happened to my voice? What had happened to my instincts? I began to swear under my breath at Virginia while I worked.

I thought Mexico would be the change of pace I needed. I had always wanted to live in Mexico, and now I had the money. Virginia thought it was a good idea. We postponed publication of my story collection. It's hard to publish a short story collection with only three stories in it.

In Mexico I set aside the work for a few weeks and melted into sun-dappled tranquility. No matter what happened, for the next year or so, I was a writer with a B&S contract, and I could talk about my editor, my award, my advance, my forthcoming book, *ad nauseam*. Even if people didn't like me (and who would?), they had to begrudgingly acknowledge that I had gone where few men, at least statistically, had ever gone before.

I liked Mexico so much I rented a big brand-new four-bedroom house, giving the owner the whole year-lease sum, seven thousand two hundred pesos, in one lump. The looks I received laying out this much cash were incredulous. This man must be rich. Well, it was true, I thought bashfully. I am so well off I can pay a sixty-dollar-a-month rent advance almost indefinitely. But then I had to renew my visa for six months, which required a return to the States. While in the U.S. I planned to tour around the country and see all my old friends before maybe disappearing into Mexico forever, as so many questionable and forgettable writers before me had done. I also thought I might drop in on Virginia at B&S in New York. Maybe we could get some things (which isn't like somethings) straightened out face-to-face where phone, e-mail, and USPS had failed us. I wrote her, and she said it sounded good.

Off I went on a thirty-day bus pass around the country. Almost immediately I got sick. In Colorado my back went out. I limped and coughed from town to town, getting weaker and more bent out of shape. At each friend's place I took to the guest bed, shivering and trying to get down some chicken soup and sleeping an extra day before I moved on to the next lucky household. I thought I'd shake the malady but I couldn't. I tried to e-mail schedule changes to my intended hosts, but due to the extra sleep days and the slowness of the bus, I was always a day or two off and had to resort to rounding off dates and calling people when I landed at the depot. After several thousand miserable miles I barely had the energy to stand out of my bus seat and crack my head on the luggage rack. I thought about packing it in, but I didn't want to give up the chance to see Virginia and maybe set our varnished boats straight.

When I landed in New York I should've gone straight to the emergency room. Instead I limped around until I found the great Burns and Sons Torture Research Center. I entered, went up the elevator, and asked to see Virginia. She was out, so I waited an hour in a small lobby. She was still out. Suspecting she was there but unwilling to see me, I left exhausted and crookedly bent like a beggar selling matches, I thought about getting a hotel so I could lie down, but there wasn't a room to be had for less than two hundred a night, and two hundred dollars will buy you more than three months in Mexico. So I crawled back to the Port Authority and called a friend, who wasn't home. The guy next to me was taking his blood pressure *phwish phwish phwish* every ten minutes. I called Burns and Sons. Virginia was still out. I called my friend, who still wasn't home. Finally, I climbed on the next bus, not even caring where it went.

Back in Mexico a month later, after I'd self-diagnosed from a Columbia University physician's manual and a trip to the *farmacia* to obtain the correct antibiotic to treat a general strep infection of a pneumococcal variety, I was well enough again to resume the Sisyphean myth with Virginia. In the meantime, even ill and barely able to walk, my embattled instincts had advised me to work independently of my esteemed editor, and with facile speed I had produced two pieces that sold immediately. The contributor's notes looked very smart: short story collection forthcoming from Burns and Sons; BASS award winner. Virginia loved the pieces (they were "terrific") but thought they could use some changes. I decided to leave the stories the way they were.

The only story Virginia and I ever collaborated on that worked at all was a piece I'd had around for about eight years about a childhood dream that connected to fear of old age and death. Virginia had some strong ideas, as usual, about how the story should be different, and I wrote it to her specifications. I think after about the fifth serious rework (it was a very short piece) she decided she liked it—except that the introduction was too much like the BASS award winner, the dream (which was a real dream and the reason I'd written the story), was trite, and the ending was not right. Some of the parts in between she thought could be cut or reworked. In other words, a three-thousand word story that I had been working on closely with her for five or six months she "liked," except for the beginning, the middle, the end, and certain parts in between.

Finally, tired of walking backward in Virginiaville, I stripped the story back as best as I could to some original, basic sensibility and sold it to Atlantic Online. Several readers wrote to tell me how weak this story seemed compared to my usual work, and how it wasn't plausible in parts. They were right. Together, as in all the stories, Virginia and I implanted plot sequences that didn't fit, added irrelevant romantic scenes, brewed hokey moral themes, applied ourselves to trivial color schemes, constructed useless motivational apparatuses, and rode the donkey the rest of the way into town only to learn that the villagers had moved on long ago.

I was on my third Mexican visa, and my savings were almost gone. I needed the second half of that royalty advance, but I wasn't any closer to finishing the manuscript than I had been on the first day. And what little material I had was so hump-backed and weird and unlike anything I would ever compose, even in a fever or after being struck in the back of the head with a pool cue, it made me ill to think of it. Another postponement was in the wings. I loathed the idea of going back to the U.S. to

get another kitchen or warehouse job. I would've worked in
Mexico if there were legitimate or legal jobs to be found, anything,
say, that paid more than the going rate of seven pesos (about
seventy cents) per hour.

One morning I was taking coffee with my American friends
at the Hotel Jardin when a young man stuck his head in the door
and asked if any of us would be interested in teaching English.
The other Americans, all retired, engaged him in a polite but disinterested exchange of information. Roberto, or Tito, as he
was called, was the husband of the owner of the nearby language
school, whose students were demanding at least one native
speaker on staff. Polite and wry declines followed all around, but
I said, why don't I give it a try?

One reason I had come to Mexico was to learn Spanish.
Like most Americans in a foreign country, however, I clung pretty
tightly to my own ethnic island. And though I studied nightly
in a very good book called *Madrigal's Magic Key to Spanish* (illus-
trations by Andy Warhol), which begins with past tense, I was
making unremarkable progress. Whenever I walked into a store
or tried to have a casual conversation with a Spanish speaker,
I was usually greeted with a horrified look, signaled to wait, and
after a few moments of hasty scuffling presented with some
poor soul who spoke English. Children who came to my door to
ask if I wanted trash taken out seemed to think I was particularly funny as I attempted to engage them in any dialogue beyond
sí or *no, gracias*. Teaching English not only paid a whopping
two dollars an hour, it also allowed me to interact with Spanish
speakers and it got me out of that giant empty house, where I
was surrounded by piles of manuscripts scribbled upon by a well-
meaning but wicked lunatic and where time passed more slowly
than all the Sunday schools put together.

Teaching English turned out to be the best way to learn Spanish. Growing up in San Diego, I'd taken Spanish classes in
school, worked in plenty of kitchens with Mexicans, and spoken
some kind of ragtag Español most of my life. But living in

nontourist agricultural Mexico six hundred miles from the border you need more than thirty-two words and seven pet
phrases, chief among them *cómo se dice*. To teach English I had
to learn Spanish grammar and all the elemental vocabulary
I'd glazed over before: through, about, unless, around. Hour after
hour I had to explain, in Spanish, why a pronoun inserted itself
here, but not there, and why the verb tense did not change with
an auxiliary. If the pupil (or the teacher) didn't understand
something, we repeated the lesson until it was clear.

Before I realized it, I was among the natives, sitting on a
park bench, standing in a doorway smoking a cigarette, at a bar
or a restaurant, making lame jokes and asking ridiculous but
syntactically correct questions or fending off someone trying to
sell me a "genuine Rolex." I was invited to dinner, to chess,
and to bed. I learned where to buy the best mangoes, *chicharrónes*,
tamales, the best meat, the best *menudo*. Cheaper rental oppor-
tunities opened to me. If I needed something fixed, a special deal,
a prescription perhaps, protection if it was required, these
doors opened as well. I met my students after hours to help them
pass their tests. I began to date one of my students. This part of
me I had honestly thought was dead.

Meanwhile, back at the bloody grindstone, Virginia and I
worked on my stories until they wore out or fell to pieces. I'd
been confidently sending out these mutually composed pieces
with cover letters that read: "I have worked with my editor
from Burns and Sons (short story collection forthcoming) on this
one and I'm pretty sure it can't be topped." The story usually
came back without a comment. Even the *Sun*, my old standby,
showed little interest in these co-authored compositions.

Since I had been selling stories for years without Virginia's
help, and since every labor between us had fallen through the
grate, I was finally forced to conclude that Virginia—a manic perfectionist with a modern college perspective who didn't know
what she was doing or why—was not in my best interests. The

little voice in my head that always knew when it was time to go said, Time to go.

But like a starving dog with its head stuck in a garbage pail or a stupid monkey with only one banana, I couldn't give up the B&S contract, and Virginia knew it. At my wit's end, I sought counsel from a few trusted friends.

Fire her, they said.

Fire her?

Yeah, get a new editor. Everyone does that.

It sounded like a smart move: if you're standing next to a bubbling pot of sulfur and some lady with red eyes is handing you a quill dipped in blood, you ain't in heaven. But I gave it a couple more months, just in case Virginia fell off Mount Vesuvius, plugged her curling iron in backward, or married a revivalist preacher. At two dollars an hour my meager savings continued to dwindle, and if I wanted to stay in Mexico the second part of that contract money was the only thing saving me from the factory.

But those packages with the penciled outlines and the hooks and little carefully scribed Beelezebubian comments in the corners kept on coming. It was like being in college all over again and doing an endless term paper on Beowulf. Virginia had me where she wanted me. Unknown and untested with that five-thousand-dollar carrot dangling in front of my eyes, she knew I wouldn't quit. And I knew she wouldn't visit me in the insane asylum. But it had gotten to the point where the drone and grit and smash of the factory would've been exhilarating compared to staring into and rewriting from her notes.

Finally in June I wrote to Virginia and said that we were incompatible, that nothing we had written together had worked. I tried to be nice. I was courteous, which is a mistake in the business world. In business lay the blame elsewhere, be the aggressor, exploit the innate weakness of your competitor, raise some hell, and ask to see the manager. Remember, you're a temperamental artist. But I didn't feel much like an artist. I told her I wanted a new editor or out of the contract.

I think Virginia, not wanting to share responsibility for our failure to produce, simply told her supervisor that I had pulled the plug. And I had been expendable from the beginning. They released me from the contract and waived the five-thousand-dollar advance, unless another publisher picked up the story collection, in which case I would have to refund the money. Virginia and I wished each other luck and never spoke again.

Mumbling regret, cursing myself, rolling my eyes heavenward every four minutes, I went back to the States and got a job in a pallet factory, then a sheet-metal house, then a cheese factory. The big publishing-house experience was so unpleasant I vowed I would never do it again, though it's true that without the B&S advance I never would have made it to Mexico, never would have learned to speak a rudimentary, functional Spanish, never would have found that mango, that *menudo*, or that mariachi band, probably never would have had a date (you can't imagine how much that was like rising from the dead). Eventually I even found another publisher, small press this time, no yellow phobia or three-page letters on how to write. No short story collection either (how could I afford it much less unravel it?). So here's to bad backs, rough luck, long bus trips, late starts, and incompatible editors, or as my grandmother used to say before she planted her annual blue-ribbon begonias, "Get out of the way, honey, it's time to spread some manure!"

Wide-Eyed
in the Gaudy Shop

A man is not complete until he is married.
Then he is finished.

ZSA ZSA GABOR

AT A BACKYARD BARBECUE UNDER THE TANGLED MES-
quite trees in this run-down but very amicable home, Victor,
one of my fellow teachers at the *Instituto de Ingles*, insists that
there is nothing in the States for me, no reason for me to return.
I know it, I admit, but Mexico is not my country; I can't go on
pretending. Besides, I'm broke and my visa is up. On the *parrilla*
Victor grills pork chops marinated in orange juice, garlic, and
beer, along with *anchos* and *helote*, chiles and corn on the cob.
His two dogs run in mindless circles around the great shady
yard with its crumbling stone walls. Victor was born here in this
small valley Mexican town, but his family moved to L.A. before
he can remember; his father was a truck driver who worked hard
and died young, but before that they used to come back here every summer. Comfortable as Victor might be here, as many people
as he knows, as fluent as he may be in Spanish, he has always
been American at heart: Eric Clapton, Double-Double In-N-Out
Burgers, the Buffalo Bills (Thurman Thomas was his man),
separation of church and state, and I am the only one in his circle
who can satisfactorily discuss these areas of nostalgia with him,
plus we talk a lot about his favorite subject, women, our mutual
students especially. He's amused that I like the dark ones, he
the light ones. He's dark (he likes to point out), I'm light.

Victor married twice in the U.S., taught in various L.A.
public high schools; lost two houses in two divorces; got tired of
the traffic jams, the gangs, the drugs, the incivility, the cost of

living, the relentless individualism; and finally moved back here, where he lives in one of his mom's five houses (she also has two in L.A.) with a local girl he intends to marry. Despite his matrimonial flops, civil-sanctioned union is still one of the anchors in his triumvirate of happiness, along with fire (as he turns another marinated chop on the grill) and dog. You oughta get yourself a wife, he says to me each time we meet, and each time he makes the case for the servile, steady, faithful Mexican woman over her implacable masculine American counterpart of ceaseless acquisition who files for divorce, takes your house, and can't even make the Guess Who happy.

I can't begin to explain my situation, not to Victor anyway, nor to any of his Trumpeting Army of the Eternally Optimistic but Usually Flat-Tired Matchmakers. Because, though I've had my share of normal romantic periods in my life, and I dream of picket fences and pudd'n in the evening as much as anyone, I've never really understood how people could stay together. Going steady as a youngster was mind-boggling in its ability to create anxiety. Proms and more serious courting patterns later were most always salvaged (and then savaged) by drugs and alcohol. I haven't found the "right one" for thirty years. Not close. I'm forty-four, and unless you're talking about some kind of Sun City shuffleboard-and-square-dancing arrangement, I'm not long past the usual age of marriageability, I'm one-leg-in-the-friggin'-grave past it. Many of my contemporaries already have grandchildren.

I do tell Victor, however, as I tell all my nosy matchmaker friends, that even if I'm not altogether opposed or closed to the possibility of a lifesaving amorous adventure strolling in while I'm having my grapefruit and coffee, I'm not so lonely or horny or discontented that I would take a foreign bride. I doubt that marriage, exotic or otherwise, would have any other effect than to complicate my malaise. I'm fiddle-footed, insecure, inclined to depressions; I sleep in odd fits; I have lost all patience with myself. Often I wish I would die just so I could run down that white tunnel of judgment and kick God in the balls, and I say this right out loud in a variety of perversely imaginative forms. I don't need a housekeeper or a loyal companion who will become annoyed at how I chew my potatoes. I've been doing my own housework since I moved out of my parents' home at age seventeen. My once strong and steady sexual appetite has atrophied over the years into a kind of thankful dormancy that I don't care to reawaken for the purposes of satisfying a set of lowbrow Bee Gees platitudes. I'm dead and I like it that way, at least it gives me more time in the evenings to read. Frankly, I think it's sad that a man could be so lonely that he'd have to go to another country to find a girl.

Twenty-two days before my visa expires as I'm standing in the doorway of the *Instituto*, here comes one of the students, Cristina, across the street, tight red sweater, the sun doing tricks on her hair. I've admired her a dozen times from afar but we've never talked. She's never been in one of my classes. Though she is busty she strives with her metal specs for an academic look. She is the head librarian played by Jane Russell. She also reminds me (the slight incisor spaces, the clapping eyelashes and labored bashful smile) of a girl I slept with a whole summer long ago.

For the first time, she is my student tonight, strange luck that. I have only two students in that class, both hoping to pass onto advanced status. I don't like either of their chances. We have fun, though, my classmates and I. I give them my best. My lessons are unconventional. Since the goal for most students is to live and work in America, I put them there: in a store, in a rental office, in front of an employer, at a car dealership. We play games: the bus has dropped you off three miles from home, the cashier has given you the wrong change, there's a sale and all the hand-bags are half off. Can you tell me where Oxnard is? Can you say Shick-oɢ-go (not cʜᴇᴇ-coggo)? Instead of useless textbook phrases such as "Will you have my trousers pressed by Monday?" I teach them utilitarian indispensables:

I need to rent an apartment.
I'm looking for a job.
Let's go out for burgers, then we'll go to Wal-Mart.
The car needs to be fixed again. We should've bought a Toyota.
Duck! He's got a gun!
Get out of my way.
You asshole, why don't you learn how to drive?
I'm going to sue you.
I'd like a lottery ticket, please.

As I regard Cristina in my classroom, I feel as if I've been drugged. I'm aware of the arsenal of potent tricks at lust's disposal, nevertheless this has an altogether different feel, per-haps I should use the word atmosphere. We happen to leave together, and I offer to walk her home. On the way I suggest we have coffee somewhere. OK, she says. Where? *Bizarro*, she says, citing the wacky artists' café six blocks south and west, where we drink coffee and trade pasts. In this motley bohemian club deco-rated like a fun house, paintings by local artists hanging from the walls, *mezclado* dance pop and Pink Floyd on the box, the pa-trons playing cards, backgammon, Chinese checkers, and chess, I think it rather ominous that our table is made from a bed. She is a courteous young woman, good eye contact, a bit intimidated, perhaps, to be dining with the maestro, but easy to talk to, even if her English is poor. A typical student, she's been dabbling for nine years, one school to the next, and she thinks that through the mere exercise of attending language school she will absorb English without having to work at it, as maybe one in three hundred adults can do. She plans to take the test to gra-duate to the advanced level in two weeks. Not a chance. I tell her I'll help her, which means another "date" tomorrow. I haven't been on a "date" since I can remember. Are pretenses to help students really "dates?" Oh, well, nothing will come of this—how could it—though my socks and brain are full of helium, even the haziest suicidal inclination has veered off like a wildfire to the east, I've forgotten all about the *el crappo* job waiting for me in the U.S. And what is this peculiar rustling in my loins like a paper flower unfolding? She's a dentist, by the way. Imagine dating a woman you can't afford to see. I don't tell her I'm leaving in twenty-two days.

Our second date begins with cakes and ale at the Café Azul, a more sedate club with fifty-foot Casablanca ceilings and almost exclusively English music on the stereo. I'm shocked that Cristina likes Echo and the Bunnymen. Another point in her favor: unlike almost every other Mexican I know she is punctual. She also insists on paying, and though you might say, Well of course she's a dentist, we make about the same hourly wage. Cristina's diffident reserve, her regal sadness, appeal to me. I wonder if it is the same sadness as mine: much sorrow, as you know, comes from poor hands dealt by Cruel Affection. But she has a good excuse for not having a mate: they've all gone to America to work. And she's still eligible, though she's running out of time. No wonder Cristina's two big dreams are to learn English and see the USA. That's where all her suitors are. I walk her home, taking the outside as we used to do with our girl-friends thirty years ago in case gangsters came rumbling down the street spraying their machine guns at the trees. No, it's called chivalry, a mocked institution in the USA, where all men are slobs and women barely have the patience to civilize them. I have this strange combination of hunger, sympathy, and paternity for her. Eighteen years my junior, I really have no busi-ness with Cristina, yet in a very short time we seem to have formed some kind of bond. On the walk in front of her house while her dog scratches and snorts on the other side of the metal gate we arrange another "date."

In the evenings I'm eager to see Cristina walking in her white jacket out of the *Clinica Dental del Oro*. My feelings cannot be a blossom of loneliness for I have lived too long alone, I'm too good at it, and I have no real desire to incinerate myself in another foolhardy liaison. She should be wary too. She has confessed that the men in her life always leave her, she doesn't know why. Perhaps this explains our cautious, low-key bearing, our reluctance to touch (by now the pose of "studying" has expired): there is so little expectation from either side, we are both so accustomed to being let down, and so close to the end of our respectable time frames, she on the brink of a devout spinsterhood, me wondering whether it will be assisted or long-term care, that it might as well be over. Yet in a land where time is friendly, disappointment is expected, and tragedy has ruled since Cortez scraped his first merchant ship upon the Mesoamerican shore, there's really nothing to lose, so why shouldn't two refugees enjoy each other's company for whatever brief time remains?

Only thirteen days left: we sit in Cristina's parlor under an oversized religious oil painting, her growling playful poodle Zeus jumping in and out of my lap, as if I were in some Third World version of *Mayberry R.F.D.* I've just met her family, her skinny dental-school brother, and two grinning beautiful sisters, one an accountant, the other getting a computer degree. Macho Papa is commensurate to a high school principal. Mother is a traditional hand-wringing financially cloistered sweetheart. In their expressions I see that I have stolen their daughter's heart; I have rescued her from ignominy; we are going to have twelve white sons who will all be pitchers for the Toronto Blue Jays. Boy, if they could just talk a little slower. Then my *novia latina* and I walk the jasmine-and-orange-blossom-scented streets to the only theater in town (she pays), where we watch a Spanish film about heroin and transvestites, the third Spanish movie about transvestites I've seen this year.

Later, on the brink of departure, I show Cristina how to use a computer and get her an e-mail account with Yahoo! so that we can correspond while I'm gone. I've suggested that I might return. I think that romantic feelings are often produced to avoid obligations such as growing up or going somewhere you don't really want to go, but I still feel it, this tugging in my stomach and rush of ringing hayseed pleasure that I have not known for a long time. I dread the thought of returning to America. If I stay, though, let my visa expire, as many expats have done, I might have trouble getting out.

Lying sleepless in bed one night an idea sprouts wildly in my mind: why not take Cristina with me? She's lonely and bored here, and though she is *La Doctora*, a woman of prestige, she's chained for a pittance six days a week to a chair owned by an overlord in the capital city who will keep her indentured as long as he can. The concept of women working en masse in the professional ranks in Mexico is fairly new, part social evolution, and—since most of the men have left and many have no desire to return to dollar-an-hour jobs—part necessity. But the women are easier to channel and manipulate, to browbeat and under-pay; they are more content to live with their parents, to resign to the church, to accept a courtyard life of dresses and shoes, and thus to sustain the magic dancing aristocracy. But if Cristina just had five thousand dollars she could open her own *consul-torio*. And if her English were serviceable, all the gringo business, the cash root-canal crop, even Canadians drifting down for 65 percent savings (dental coverage for adults under retirement age is not part of the social package there) would line up at her door. And since I have no other obligations outside of supporting tobacco taxes, the metered flushing of a toilet, and filling a modest casket soon, this could be exciting, even useful, even who knows what?

The night I announce to Cristina that I'm willing to take her to America with me she regards me with the mouth movements and glass-eyed bugginess of a goldfish. She's convinced I'm jok-ing. I explain my plan, which revolves around five grand. She seems upset now. *Qué gacho!* she says. I don't want money. I want us. Of course not, I sputter. I only meant. But look, we'll be together. We'll travel and point at mountains and billboards, dip our tater tots into the same ketchup, and see how harmonious we are. The famous American test-drive. Who knows what will happen? I can't give you any guarantees, but let's see how we do together. Oh, my Spanish really begins to suck when I'm backed into a corner. Cristina says she will talk to her parents.

The answer is Yes! Wow, that was quick. Cristina already has a tourist visa, which I'm convinced would've expired unused had I not appeared. Her parents regard me as if they may have me canonized in the church. Of course I'm happy too, though a single question has begun to plague my mind: what the hell am I doing?

Well, too late to turn back now. I'm good for my word, what else have I got? Besides, I want to do one worthwhile thing on this planet before I hang up my hat. This excellent young woman has dreams and I hold the cards even casually to make every one of them come true. And her father has given her the equivalent of TWO THOUSAND DOLLARS, which looks frighteningly like a dowry. But don't you worry, Papa (he does seem a bit relieved to get one of his three unmarried daughters out of the house, now that I think about it), I'm an honorable man. We're going to make this work. You're not going to be disappointed. Even if we don't live happily ever after Cristina's going to have her own *consultorio*, free bridges and crowns for the family, and she'll be able to order competently off an English menu, her virtue intact. If not, then how does a new fishing boat with sonar and a seventy-five-gallon holding tank sound?

Tonight, as we do every night, we work on her English, which refuses to improve. Cristina's not stupid, just set in her ways and, like many colonial girls, accustomed to having someone else manage her affairs. American cults and corporations dine on these types, so I'm trying to instill in her some modicum of independent thinking. She has no idea what she's getting into: fast-spinnin', hard-shuckin', blood-spittin', heavy-telemarketin', sue-your-pants-off America. I paint her realistic portraits of chronically unhappy tattooed people permanently glued to their cell phones. Cristina doesn't believe me. She knows the streets of America are paved with gold.

I've always been proud of my spontaneity, the fact that every year I'm some place I would've never guessed the year before, but this, boarding a plane with a woman I barely know, in complete charge of her, a virgin no doubt, a dentist, a devout Catholic who barely speaks English, a woman who doesn't drive, who has never eaten peanut butter, who doesn't know who John Wayne, Bob Dylan, or Franklin Delano Roosevelt are, who has never seen a real elephant or giraffe, never even been on an airplane—well, now that's stretching even my definition of spontaneity.

BORDERLAND AMERICA IS nearly indistinguishable from Borderland Mexico: they are opposite shores of the same lagoon swapping the same trashy tide. Cristina is reluctant to speak English. I think she is uncomfortable but at the same time excited and confused as her romantic notions of the U.S. crash against the rusted, littered shore. After we clear customs my parents meet us on the other side of the border. Though they don't show it, they must be astonished by my decision to bring this foreign girl home. It can only look to them like matrimony. They are familiar with Cristina through my correspondence and are aware of my plans to help her. And though I suppose they would like to see me married, even under slightly modified cultural (see desperate) circumstances, I would like to assure them there is small possibility of this. I am not one of those pitiful fellows who needs a mail-order bride. I may look like a lonely joker grasping at straws, but I have a plan.

Cristina has a tourist visa for six months, but legally she cannot work. We are not going to stay here, in San Diego, especially with my parents, for many reasons, chiefly cost and the fact that everywhere she goes someone speaks fluent Spanish with her. Her English, as I've said, despite all her years in schools and the work we do together daily, is deplorable. Cristina cannot understand much of anything, even enunciated slowly. I need to find a place I can take her where she will have no

Spanish outlets, where she will be forced to learn English. Immersion, in my opinion, is the only school. It won't be fun, but having granted dream number one, it's the only way we can fulfill dream number two. And then we need to get her a job.

Before the harsh reality of jobs for both of us sets in, however, we enjoy ourselves for a short time with my parents. Cristina's eyes shine when I take her to the ocean, but when I take her to the mall that's when they really sparkle. California is too much, all these places to shop, a dreamland especially if you make more than a hundred a week. Although I say it isn't necessary, Cristina finds a shop full of gaudy items and falls in love with acrylic paperweights full of floating coins, glitter, tiny dice, and playing cards, and buys one for my mom. It's worth the trip just to see her thoughtfulness and how wide-eyed she is in the gaudy shop. I wish I felt slightly less like a scientist. I do love Cristina though, don't get me wrong, and I have not forgotten for a second that I really have no idea what I'm doing.

On Sundays I drive Cristina to the nearest Catholic church, where they have the dried-up, sparsely attended English Mass at ten (it's the Catholics turn to play the heavy in the new millennium), then the juicy SRO Spanish-speaking Mass (where the Catholics are still the good guys) at one, the church packed with three hundred or so Latinos. She's not crazy about this church, which looks more like a sculpture you might see in a park in San Francisco. "Catholic," of course means "universal," but they do things pretty differently here, and there is an artsy crucifixion sculpture hanging above the altar that might be a rendition of a Norwegian Olympic skiing hero. In Cristina's great ancient traditional colonial palace of a sanctuary back home a towering golden statue of Mother Mary resides above all.

It isn't just the churches that don't past muster. Americans are zombies, Cristina declares, (zombie being the same word in both languages). Americans are cold. Americans are like robots (robot is also the same word—see how easy it is to speak another language?). I feel offended. I leap to the defense of my countrymen. I can make fun of them, they're my people, but we're lining you up the number one blue plate special, American Dream with fries on the side, so think twice, child, about these cavalier remarks. Also, consider how distant people might seem when you can't understand what they are saying. Also, realize that fully half the people who live in this state have recently come (many at the risk of jail and death) from your country. And, it won't be long, if things work according to plan, before you're attached to a cell phone, butterfly-tattooed ankle laid up on knee, Xanax kicking in, bargaining with the newest credit card company over that sudden outlandish jump in your APR.

Compounding her culture shock, Cristina has to learn about the real me, not a tall rich *gringo pacifico* salvaging her humdrum life, but a guy with very little money and not much prospect who's never stayed anywhere with anyone for very long. We walk along the cloudy beach for four miles from Belmont Park to Crystal Pier, and I tell her all my crazy beach stories, which only make her frown as if the sun were in her eyes. My past is so wild it appears to have been lived by Peter Pan sniffing airplane glue. I tell Cristina she can go home whenever she wants, no hard feelings. She still has plenty of money. Cristina tells me she will think about it.

In the meantime, she has news from home that her poodle Zeus is misbehaving in her absence and that her mother and two sisters are going to Puerto Vallarta. Cristina wants to go too. She has a bad case of homesickness. I keep expecting her to say, "I want to go back," and I am prepared emotionally: what would've once been a cluster of lightning-bolt panic is now a feeling like an avocado pit in my stomach. She is strong in her way and me in mine—though I don't imagine we are anymore suited for each other than the average tourist and her guide.

Despite all her qualms and reservations, Cristina announces she will go with me, wherever I decide. I am the reason she is here. How anyone could think that is a little beyond me, a sign of weakness or lunacy, though I imagine a very simple and satisfying life with her. I ask her where she'd like to go and show her the places on the map. The USA might be Jupiter to her. Cristina doesn't know where New York is, Texas, New Orleans. Idaho is just a funny sound.

I have been offered my old nightmare cooking spot in Chadron, Nebraska, where I lived long ago for only a few months and every year since they have contacted me and asked me to work the summer, usually at a decent wage with a free room in the hotel upstairs. I don't voluntarily seek out nightmare cooking positions, and I am reluctant to return to a place I've already lived. However, this seems the best option. So Nebraska and free quarters for the summer it is: the Nightmare Cooking Job for me and—what else?—Maid Duty for Cristina.

IT'S APRIL IN Nebraska and the steady wind coming down off the mountains across the plains is still raw. The small town is so sparsely populated, dotted with trailers and deserted houses, that it feels deserted itself. There's a Catholic church in this town, too, but Cristina doesn't attend. She wouldn't know what they were saying. And something more than words has been lost in the translation. When we first get there I try to sleep on a fold-out bed in the kitchen in our hotel room, leaving Cristina alone in the bed with her decorum, but we are lost in America now and the nominalism of custom combined with the Wild West looks Cristina gives me compels me to sing to you a refrain from a Charlie Rich song. I'm glad she brought her gods with her. Mine are more like modern American parents, drifted off in the pursuit of their own cosmic interests. But I promised her I would say no more, divulge no more of our intimate secrets. I am a public confessor. My secrets are magic coins I give to my readers for their long walks through the lonesome forests. Cristina is a private confessor, a classy orthodox woman, so when we get behind closed doors, and she lets her hair hang down, you'll just have to wait out in the hall. Sorry.

The first day at work Cristina gets her first close look at one

of these new-fangled contraptions, a vacuum cleaner, and has
the same problem I always do: how the hell do you turn it on? Without an oven, and in no financial position to eat out frequently,
we assemble cold lunches and microwave: canned chow mein,
ravioli, black-eyed peas. She has her first Caesar salad, her first
pastrami-and-Swiss, her first fudge brownie. We drink red wine.
We listen to C D s (the Wallflowers and Toad the Wet Sprocket
will always remind me of this time). I smoke out in the hall looking out over the wide snow-dusted prairie and wonder what in
heaven's name I have done.

Until summer we are about the only tenants in the hotel, so
not much work for Cristina, though she does get to examine the
most private details of the occasional guest: the itinerant salesman, the parole officer, the B I A agent, the truck driver, and the
Church of Christ missionary with his suitcase full of miniature
liquor bottles and bag of mysterious white powder. At three
thirty every afternoon I leave her to work my shift. Cristina is so
far from home she might be in Greenland. There is no one to
talk to. She studies, plays with her Franklin talking dictionary, ar-
ranges her belongings, and watches the snow blow across the
single high window and the screen of the tiny black-and-white T V.

After a few weeks in the hotel, a friend offers us a house
rent-free till the end of summer. It is a dark, small house, only two
bedrooms, one small enough to be a closet, the north side
windowless on account of the battering winds coming off the
high plains day and night. There is a small fireplace so inefficient
that it is actually colder in the house with a fire going, and the
flaming logs occasionally tumble down onto the carpet—wa-
hooo!—now all I need is a dog to complete my triumvirate of happiness, isn't that right, Victor?

Cristina is suffering from culture shock and homesickness
and I tell her things will get better. A washer and dryer, something her mother has never known, and all the other modern con-
veniences such as toasters and thermostats, do nothing to
improve her disposition. Cæsar salads, rock music, and Ameri-

can movies: *tampoco* (neither). We both sleep a great deal in this dark house across from the railroad tracks. We talk, take long walks, and lie on the futon that we've dragged into the living room and placed in front of the fireplace because the back bedroom would be a better place to raise penguins. A garter snake occasionally flickers up the hot-water pipe in the bathroom and Cristina flees, shouting, *Vibora! Vibora!*

Deracinated from her gentle soil, her language, her religion, Cristina feels as if she is losing her identity. Over and over she says this, and whatever might give her comfort, her church, her saints, her American *paisanos*, they all seem to have lost their identities too. There is this ride called the American Dream, and into the whale's mouth glide the motorboat hopefuls, but out the other side emerge figures sodden and grotesque, hard-eyed, a cynical twist at the corner of their mouths. Cristina has always dreamt of entering this tunnel, but now she resists, even if she can make fifteen bucks an hour as a dental assistant.

All I can do is stay by Cristina's side and remind her how difficult change is. I tell her how grandiosely I have been lost myself, most of my life in another place, learning a new language, a new set of people and rules. But you were in your own country, she counters. Not always, and even then it often didn't seem so. But I am of little help. So we play Yahtzee, and we drink, and we eat well in front of the fire. Just about everything I prepare—yams, chard, mashed potatoes, mushrooms, barbecued ribs, blueberry muffins, sloppy joes, grilled cheese sandwiches, salmon steaks, hash browns, catfish, waffles, jambalaya, lasagna, gravy—is new to Cristina. Accustomed to soda-pop wine, she begins to appreciate the dark cheap reds from which my platelets are composed. She smokes with me, guiltily, even greedily, for the same reasons: those surges of well-being are so hard to find in nature on their own.

In July, Cristina's visa almost up, we convene at the table to decide which direction each of us will go. A dearth of work for her and a few unexpected expenses have left us with less money than we planned. Another six-month travel visa soon for Cristina is unlikely, and I don't want her working illegally anymore. Because we have been living as husband and wife, I feel I have no other choice than to marry her. I don't know if we're compatible; we've hardly had time for anything but keeping her from the brink of sorrow. Marry her, advises the woman who owns the hotel. Marry her, echoes my friend who has given me this house. You won't find a better girl. Miserable as Cristina may be, lacking in self-confidence, a veritable Helen Keller to my Anne Sullivan, there is no denying her qualities, her solid sweetness, practical intelligence, loyalty, excellent work habits (Zacatecanos are renowned for their work ethic), and those cupid lips. And much as she hates America, she is filling this house with plants, prints, pots, clothes, candles, curtains, rugs, an aquarium. Cristina has grown fond of the television show *The Jeffersons*. Peanut butter has finally cast its spell over her.

Marrying Cristina might be my last chance to be a man. Is it really, after all these years, not too late? Admittedly I am also caught up in the lure of a sedentary life, not having to pack up my junk and go off to some strange place to convince the mayor, the dogcatcher, and the village idiot that I am not on the lam and not having to nail sticks together or solder mirrors onto iron fish heads by the dirty river until I have enough money to leave. If I stay here, I could collect my notebooks and manuscripts, begin the long-haul concentration on a novel; I could for once enjoy the reputation of being a good neighbor, and I won't have to go out and get a lousy job because I already have one!

But what do you want to do, Cristina? It's up to you.

She begins to cry, and who wouldn't given the choice between returning home with nothing and marrying me?

The night before we are to be married at the county courthouse she dreams her house back in Mexico has burned down. I tell her it represents a break from the past. She looks at me seriously. I tell her it is a good dream. *Tiene que crecer*. You have to grow. You have to leave and say good-bye.

The Irving

IN THE SMALL NEBRASKA TOWN WHERE I LIVE, I AM known as "The Cook." Even people I don't know will often stare at me fuzzily for a moment before that relieved flash of recognition. Hey, I know you, you're "The Cook." Which is reasonable enough, I suppose, since I am the cook. It isn't exactly what I've dreamed of all my life, however. Actually being a cook is a sort of unpleasant byproduct of all my efforts to be "The Writer."

But recently, out of the blue, I was invited to a literary festival, held in Portland, Oregon, called Wordstock, in which I was to be "The Writer"—a small fry flitting through the nets after the big ones were already landed, yes, and then of course my publisher, who'd arranged a dinner for Russell Banks, thought I should be "The Cook," but I was flattered nonetheless.

Not long after I had bought a blazer from a thrift store for sixteen bucks (I don't think it looked too bad, it was rust brown, I hadn't worn one for twenty years), I began to formulate a plot to punch a celebrity in the nose. If you only get a chance to make a splash every ten or fifteen years you should make a big splash. Norman Mailer was slated to appear at this festival, along with Russell Banks, as I said, John Irving, Alice Sebold, Jean Auel (selling her cans of cave bear, or her caved-in beer cans, or whatever they are), and many other authors I didn't particularly admire. The publishing business is as stuffy and fickle as any other form of show business, built on name recognition, cronyism, aggressive agents, formula, titillation, what sold yesterday, and the most bulldogged, tawdry, and shameless stunts the PR team can dream up. If you believe the blurbs, there are more "geniuses" working today in the publishing business than in the Renaissance, the Jazz Age, and the Manhattan Project all put together. "Literature," with the help of the academies and the knit-browed and coldhearted literary journals, has come to be agreed upon by the general public as something akin to vitamins, dry and difficult to swallow, but good for us somehow.

Which is one of the many reasons I've never finished school. I've always thought that "literature" should be interesting, funny if possible, not lighthearted or insubstantial or in want of nutrition, by any means, but built top-to-bottom to be read. The crafty magpies who captain American industry have a bottom line to think of, however, and they know what makes the mare go. They understand that most people don't drink beer, they drink advertising. They don't drive cars, they drive advertising. They don't vote for a candidate, they vote for advertising. Books are no different. You have to tell people what they want. Otherwise you'll have to actually make a product that isn't Budweiser, Chevrolet, or George W. Bush. As long as America clings to the primacy of fame and surrenders its reality to the designers of mass cult consumption, this is how it will remain. If readers got the notion that books should actually be interesting, not difficult, dry, or ambiguous, who knows what kinds of calamities might befall the economy? There are forty thousand magazines to fill, a new novel published every half an hour, MFAs hatching like mayflies. Why tantalize consumers with red mangoes when all you've got is canned corn?

My plot began to run along these lines: everyone—us anyway, the have-nots, who make up 90 percent of the population—loves a revolution; a big party; free stuff; a chance to get out of the house, get off work; the stiff, stale, and corrupt falling under the wheels of progress; the illusion of change; new blood rising to the top. Let's kick all the stuffed lions down the stairs and shovel these old mastodon carcasses to the side of the road. Boston Tea Party! Martin Luther! Madame Lafarge! Down with tsarist Russia (leave your vodka, though)! And why shouldn't I be the one to light the fuse?

So I reckoned that if I punched Norman Mailer in the nose at some high-profile event, just stepped up to the podium and laid him flat, camera bulbs popping, as he had done to Gore Vidal many years ago (or so the legend goes), maybe I could pave the way for the New Regime. I'm talking about Us again, you and me, the rejected, jilted, oppressed, ignored, got-off-to-a-late-start, the small fries, can't land an agent, missed-the-boat prodigies, the unknown geniuses, the readers who spend all day at the library and can't find a single thing to read except biographies of Thomas Jefferson and exposés of Ronald Reagan's hemorrhoids. The Have-Nots. Give the unlucky another roll of the dice! Get out of the way you old dust bags. Us!

I understood that Norman was old, eighty-two (several of my friends wrote me before I left: is he still alive?), but this was an even better reason to help him along. He'd recently been paid two point five million dollars from the University of Texas for nine hundred boxes of "crap" (did I say "crap?" I meant "papers"), ranging from manuscripts to canceled checks to car repair bills. Car repair bills? Imagine being able to sell your fookin' car repair bills. "With love and trepidation," he sold his car repair bills for two point five million smackers. Think of how many interesting writers two point five million dollars could support. The old fossil deserved a pop. And he'd gotten to bray about his bloated opinions for fifty years. Granted, he's a monumental intellect who writes well about murder and war, but he has the soul of a Korean alarm clock. What beauty has he wrought? How many times has he made me laugh or filled me with the wonder of being human? He's as dry as leftover turkey. He'll be utterly forgotten by next Monday. And I thought, Even if I never achieve acclaim as a man of letters I will no longer be known as "The Cook," but as the guy who punched the U Tex Car Bill Dust Bag and started the revolution. "Our novels no longer weigh four pounds or read like car repair bills thanks to Poe Ballantine." (P.S. Hope you get out of federal prison soon.)

But then, just before my flight reservations were confirmed, I learned that I would be opening for John Irving. I was awestricken. It certainly had to be a fluke. But it was apparently not a fluke. The event was going to be televised by C-SPAN, the incredible blue-sky news continued, and thousands of people would not only attend, but pay to attend. And John Irving is a pop star, Captain Quirk, fluffy as the whipped pink sugar at the county fair. He opens supposedly serious novels with sentences like "In the hospital of the orphanage—the boys' division at St. Cloud's, Maine—two nurses were in charge of naming the new babies and checking that their little penises were healing from the obligatory circumcision." Captain Quirk has learned the art of keeping his reader's attention with penises and spilled semen and women fellating horses. Piggy Sneed and Owen Meany indeed. No, destiny had stepped in to direct me. Punching an eighty-two-year-old man who had spoken out early and vehemently against the Vietnam War, even if he's one of the great sand dunes of our era, would get me no sympathy at all.

Quirk was my man. And I was going to be on stage with him, live cameras rolling, the revolution like a spark in the tight darkness of my right fist. True, Irving was an accomplished wrestler, a man still very fit for sixty-three, but he'd never know what hit him. I'd be in jail with my name splashed across the national papers before he was out of the dentist's chair. Who is this Poe Ballantine? Who is this cheesy stunt artist, this sociopathic public relations hound, this brazen hypocritical anarchist? And what are the names of his books? Yes, we're going to read this dazzling rogue, this bodacious Young Turk, this delectably lawless scoundrel. We'll buy anyone who embarrasses himself publicly, who sucks off a president, who plagiarizes for a major newspaper, who cheats at sports or business, who kills people for a living.

Rhonda, my publisher, met me at the Portland airport. A lean, energetic brunette of forty years with hip fifties-looking

wing specs, she makes her money as a print broker and then frit-
ters it away on people like me. She printed five thousand copies
of my first book, for example, and it must have sold two thousand
copies. She laughed when I told her my plan. She thought it was
a good idea. She thought I was joking, of course. All the better for
a surprise, I thought, (doing little patty-cakes in my mind).
Every one of the books on her list would soar up the charts. We'd
be like Death Row Records, swaggering brigands with samurai
tattoos and our own special hand signals, the public so frightened they'd just have to call us artists. She'd have to bail me out
of jail, yes, but what small price is that to pay for success?
And even the modest, upright people would soon forget how I
snaked my way into the limelight.

I stayed with my publisher in her fabulous ninth-floor cor-
ner loft overlooking downtown Portland and the Willamette
River. On clear days, through her green glass walls, you can see
Mount Hood, the Cascades, and the fumitory Mount St. Helens.
After I threw all my stuff into the storage room where I would sleep,
Rhonda said, "Let's go get something to eat. I'm not going to
drink, though," she added. This is what she always says. But she
was right this time. We had a busy week ahead. The big reading,
"The Irving," as she had begun to call it, was tomorrow. We walked
down the street to the Rogue for hamburgers. One beer with
a hamburger is not drinking, so we had just one more pint. And
then we went down the block for habanero martinis—have you
tried those? they don't have them where I'm from: vodka infused
with habanero peppers shaken with pineapple juice over ice
and poured fizzing into a martini glass rimmed with sugar—not
exactly a martini, but speaking of brazen public exhibitions,
quite the little punch in the kisser. Let's have another. We were
glowing by the time we got home and decided to drink wine and
finally we got to bed about two that morning.

I slept on a futon surrounded by books, many of them mine,
boxes and boxes of unsold books by "The Cook" in that dark
storage room with its exposed ducts and roaring central-air fan.

It was as dark as the cave of a clan bear in there. I couldn't see anything, not even the clock. I had to feel my way for the light switch. It was terrific, utter peace. I felt like a lion in its lair.

In the morning I was badly hungover with tachycardia that convinced me I would die before I ever got the chance to slug anyone. I slept in late. I don't normally drink much, but how many days out of the year do I get to be "The Writer?" And how long before I'd be sent to a place where cocktails were prohibited? When my heart stopped thrashing around, I had to concentrate on how I would punch John Irving. Left-handed, right? Straight jab, uppercut? Give him a slight warning? Perhaps make an arrangement with him so he could dive? I didn't want to hurt him. I only needed to articulate the symbol, supply the image. Later I would be interviewed, be labeled crazy or whatever, but I'd tell them just what I'm telling you: Literature is fusty, it's clogged, it's anal, it's winded, it's fading, it's lost its heart. It's rehash. It's a cottage industry built around the creative writing programs. It's too many goddamn historical novels. It's this third-generation immigrant writing "humorously" about the Holocaust, or this "talented" New Yorker prodigy blowing bagpipes about his supposedly daring life. In music you're only as good as your last hit. In literature one decent-selling book and we have to listen to you until they zip the coffin shut or you sell your nine hundred boxes of crap at the door of the rest home. I'm just doing my part. I'm just trying to clear the way for the ones who belong here, the ones who have something to say, the ones who are willing to give more than their "talent," the ones who have gambled and lived.

Once I recovered my normal heartbeat, took a shower, and drank a beer, I started getting nervous. In a few hours I would be reading in a giant hall in front of two thousand people. And then I was going to make a spectacle of myself, crack the plaster into that frightening chasm of anarchy in front of gentle, left wing, mostly passive scholastic people, the same ones who had started the last few American revolutions. I practiced the piece I would read, and my introduction: "Thank you for putting up with me. I'm flattered to be your wienie roll-ups, your REO Speedwagon. Nathanael West said: 'Forget the epic. Forget the masterwork. In America fortunes do not accumulate, the soil does not grow, families have no history. Leave slow growth to the book reviewers, you only have time to explode! Remember William Carlos Williams's description of the pioneer women who shot their children against the wilderness like cannonballs. Do the same with your novels!'"

My young friend Mr. Scott Nadelson, another meager-selling Hawthorne Books writer, a gloomy well-dressed man of thirty years (no thrift stores for Scott) who lives and teaches in Portland and would go first among the three warm-up readers, came over about 5:00 p.m. and we drank some fifteen-year-old Scotch to loosen up. The reading was at 7:00 p.m. We had to be there by 6:30 p.m. "What are you going to read?" I said.

"Half a story," he said, gloomily. "You know, my stories are so long. You?"

"My dead-guy chapter."

"Oh, that's a good one."

"More Scotch?"

"Just a touch."

It wasn't enough. That Pinch seemed to evaporate before it got to my lips. Oh, how I suddenly dreaded this night. I couldn't tell Scott about my plan. He didn't like Irving either, but he had recently won an Oregon Book Award. He had no need for cheap stunts. I finished my Scotch. I began to feel like a bad actor. I began to feel like John Wilkes Booth.

At six o'clock, a troop of us—writers, editors, husbands and wives of—strolled across town through the wind, all joking with nervous smiles in our snappy duds into the biggest night of our small-time literary lives. My plan had grown complicated. First, Irving was flying in late. He would not even hear his warm-ups read. He would stroll in just in time to comb his hair and have his hand kissed, read, answer a few questions, attend his fifty-dollar admission party, and be off again through the ticker tape to the powdered rosy anuses of high society. Second, the warm-up authors would read fifteen minutes each and then exit the staging area, leaving us effectively partitioned from him (as he probably requested, sensing a revolution in the wings). To get to Irving in the spotlight, I'd have to sneak and then lurk backstage, or come leaping out from the audience at some point. Maybe jump down from the balcony, as Booth had done. At least they would know who I was when they saw me. Hey, that's the guy who read earlier, "The Writer." I thought of the headlines in the paper of my small town: "Cook Attacks Beloved Writer."

The Keller Auditorium is a ballet and opera hall, children's theater, etc., that seats almost three thousand. Mister Scott and I were led to the greenroom backstage. Scott informed me that most "greenrooms" are not really green. I imagine they call them green after the complexions of their occupants, which is certainly how I felt. There were a number of people already present, writers, sponsors, organizers, a couple of introducers, a photographer, and the emcee. I shook hands and introduced myself all around.

This was my first time in a greenroom, my first time on TV, my first time meeting someone famous (though I had once seen Roger Mudd from a car window in D.C.), and my first time reading to more than thirty or forty people. I checked my bookmarks and internally mumbled my introduction. I chatted with the people backstage, especially the emcee, a friendly guy from Oregon Public Broadcasting, who with his fedora and beard reminded me of the great Bukowski. Mostly I had to explain why I was from Nebraska. I like Nebraska, actually, I ex-plained to them. I can afford to live there, for instance. The air is very clean. The people are all broke like me and except for cal-ling me "The Cook" they are congenial and often even helpful. I could've talked all day about Nebraska but it was plain that no one believed me.

The clock struck 7:00 p.m. The hour had finally arrived. The emcee strolled out and set up the first introducer, who fished about for laughs, finally found some, began to enjoy himself, and seemed to stay too long. That was all right. Each extra minute he spent out there meant one less minute of suffering for me. Then someone said, "Two minutes," and Scott, looking drained, tugged at a shirt button and was led away, as if to his execution. Fifteen minutes, I thought, and it will be my turn. Everyone says the same thing when it's their time: what about tomorrow or next week instead?

I watched Scott read on the monitor in the greenroom. The shot was from afar, fuzzy, small, and barely visible. Typical C-SPAN. It's actually what I like about C-SPAN. The whole notion of production is secondary to the event. I concentrated on Scott and his reading. He was doing well. He was used to this. He read dozens of times every year to various audiences. He'd just wrapped up this book award and had gone on a big tour to large audiences all across the country, including New York City and women throwing their room keys at him. I hadn't read much, usually "open mike," with all the other unrecognized geniuses after the professors and the paid guests had strolled back home. I was beginning to get shaky. I wondered if I would get sick. I wondered if my heart would go haywire again. I glanced at Scott on the monitor. I calculated about eight minutes before my turn.

And then John Irving entered the room. I was too busy trying to get my breathing under control to devote much attention to him. I sat there with my book in my lap. Everyone leaped to their feet. I had expected him to be somewhat arrogant. Instead he was gracious and mild. He seemed patient and wise. He didn't seem at all like a man who would indiscriminately use the word *penis* to keep his reader's attention. He wore a green shirt and light suit coat. Everyone buzzed and bustled around him. Some of these people had known him for years, some knew him in passing, others merely wanted to meet him. Out of courtesy I introduced myself. He sort of dipped his head and said, as if he were trying to remember me that night he threw the winning touchdown while I was sitting on the bench lacing up my cleats forty-eight years ago: "Ballantine."

The photographer arranged us in various poses and snapped off a few shots. I was grateful for the distraction. I was aware that the seconds continued to pass, but one form of idle stimulation had supplanted another and modified the unpleasant passage of time. I also reminded myself that, in the scheme of things, if I read well or succeeded tonight or didn't, it wouldn't make much difference. The night would shimmer away under the weight of a thousand others. And one day, if I was lucky, I would be an old man in a room with a memory of one great night with the stars.

"Two minutes," someone said, and a few people swung their heads around at me. I smiled at them and scraped all my stuff together and checked my bookmarks I felt tall and dry and green, like a bamboo plant with bamboo joints. I was led away. I heard the thunder of applause. The emcee shuffled out, did his shtick, and extended an arm. Keep it slow, I thought, shuffling out into the blazing lights and the polite applause of the audience.

I couldn't see a thing out there, not even the faint glimmer of jewelry. It was darker than the storage room where I had slept and where I would get sick after drinking too much pinot noir after cooking enchiladas for Russell Banks because I couldn't find the damn doorknob. It was perfect. I drew myself up to the podium. You could just look out into that blackness and pretend you were seeing faces, acknowledging intellects, sympathizing with hospital workers, cooks, and struggling writers. I cut my introduction in half. ("Do the same with your novels!") And leaped straight into the chapter from *God Clobbers Us All* about an eighteen-year-old acidhead surf bum who has to help an aide on her first day clean up a neglected corpse. I knew the tempo to keep it under fifteen minutes, especially with a truncated intro and a few parts snipped out here and there. I looked up frequently as I read, corner to corner, front to back.

I know this is important from watching people read. Be confi-
dent, be natural, be funny, look up. Why bore them? Be like good
Chinese food and give them something to take home.

To my surprise, they laughed. In smaller groups sometimes
people are unsure of whether it's appropriate to laugh or not, so
a very funny piece might be met as if you were speaking a foreign
language. In front of a small group, you don't ever really know
about your material. But behind the armor of their comrades,
lost in the safety of the herd, they can cut loose. And they hadn't
come to be lectured to. They hadn't come for leftover turkey.
They came to be entertained. They actually left their televisions,
their bars, and their DVD players. This is the terrible new responsibility the modern writer must now face, and "writing well,"
even if it's about Ronald Reagan's hemorrhoids, isn't enough.
They laughed so hard I had to stop reading at points, still shivering through every dendrite and anxious to come to the end.

Afterward Mister Scott and I signed a few books out in the
lobby. People approached me with a weird sparkle in their eyes
to congratulate me. Outside, the stars seemed strangely bright.
Women were all over Scott. He was even signing books outside.
Finally we broke away and sneaked back down into the audience
to hear Irving. He was an excellent reader, fluid and relaxed,
looking up often, holding his audience, making them laugh. Suddenly he seemed like a wonderful guy. I realized he had worked
hard to get where he was. It was difficult to imagine how I had
ever plotted to drop him. As I settled back into the submissive
brainlessness of contentment, I longed vaguely for my earlier
vigor to be restored. What was I now but another minion,
another hanger-on? The slightest success had robbed me of my
fire. It hadn't taken much. Later in the week, as Norman Mailer's
limo pulled up to the curb, I felt nothing as the harmless
old mastodon stepped out into the rain, even if my hours were
numbered, my glittering days soon to be forgotten, the people of
my small town waiting eagerly for me to return home and cook
them some supper.

Hawthorne Books & Literary Arts
Portland, Oregon

Current Titles

At Hawthorne Books, we're serious about literature. We suspected that good writers were being ignored and cast aside as a result of consolidation in the publishing industry, and in 2001 we decided to find these writers and give them a voice. We publish American literary fiction and narrative non-fiction, although we won't turn down a good international title if we find one. All of our books are published as affordable original trade paperbacks, but feature details not typically found even in casebound titles from bigger houses: acid-free papers; sewn bindings which will not crack; heavy, laminated covers with French flaps and built-in bookmarks. You can probably buy Hawthorne Books wherever you buy books, or from our Web site (*hawthornebooks.com*) postpaid* and for a substantial discount. If you like to read, we think you'll enjoy our books. If you like to write—well, send us something. We're always looking.

Free postage available only for orders shipped within the United States. Sorry about that.

FINALIST, 2005 OREGON BOOK AWARD

Core: A Romance
Kassten Alonso

Fiction / 208pp / $12.95 / 0-9716915-7-6

This intense and compact novel crackles with obsession, betrayal, and madness. As the narrator becomes fixated on his best friend's girlfriend, his precarious hold on sanity deteriorates into delusion and violence in this twenty-first-century retelling of the classic myth of Hades and Persephone.

"Jump through this Gothic stained-glass window and you are in for some serious investigation of darkness and all of its deadly sins. But take heart, brave traveler, the adventure will prove thrilling."
Tom Spanbauer Author of *Now is the Hour*

TITLE STORY INCLUDED
IN THE BEST AMERICAN ESSAYS 2006

501 Minutes to Christ
Poe Ballantine

Essays / 174pp / $13.95 / 0-9766311-9-9

This collection of personal essays ranges from Ballantine's diabolical plan to punch John Irving in the nose during a literary festival, to the tale of how after years of sacrifice and persistence, Ballantine finally secured a contract with a major publisher for a short story collection that never came to fruition.

"My soul yearns to know this most entangled enigma. I confess to Thee, O Lord, that I really have no idea what Poe Ballantine is talking about."
St. Augustine

Decline of the Lawrence Welk Empire
Poe Ballantine

Fiction / 376pp / $15.95 / 0-9 66311-1-3

Edgar Donahoe is back for another misadventure, this time in the Caribbean. When he becomes involved with his best friend's girl and is stalked by murderous island native Chollie Legion, even Cinnamon Jim, the medicine man, is no help—it takes a hurricane to blow Edgar out of the mess.

"This second novel ... initially conjures images of *Lord of the Flies*, but then you would have to add about ten years to the protagonists' ages and make them sex-crazed, gold-seeking alcoholics."
Library Journal

HAWTHORNE BOOKS & LITERARY ARTS

God Clobbers Us All
Poe Ballantine

Fiction / 196pp / $15.95 / 0-9716915-4-1

Set against a decaying San Diego rest home in the 1970s, *God Clobbers Us All* is the shimmering, hysterical, melancholy account of eighteen-year-old surfer-boy/orderly Edgar Donahoe, who struggles with romance, death, friendship, and an ill-advised affair with the wife of a maladjusted war veteran.

"Calmer than Bukowski, less portentous than Kerouac, more hopeful than West, Poe Ballantine may not be sitting at the table of his mentors, but perhaps he deserves his own after all."
San Diego Union-Tribune

Things I Like About America
Poe Ballantine

Essays / 266pp / $12.95 / 0-9716915-1-7

These risky personal essays are populated with odd jobs, eccentric characters, boarding houses, buses, and beer. Written with piercing intimacy and self-effacing humor, they take us on a Greyhound journey through small-town America and explore what it means to be human.

"Part social commentary, part collective biography, this guided tour may not be comfortable, but one thing's for sure: You will be at home."
Willamette Week

WINNER, 2005 I ANGIIM PRIZE FOR
HISTORICAL FICTION

Madison House
Peter Donahue

Fiction / 528pp / $16.95 / 0-9766311-0-b

This novel chronicles Victorian Seattle's explosive transformation from frontier outpost to metropolis. Maddie Ingram, owner of Madison House, and her quirky and endearing boarders find their lives linked when the city decides to regrade Denny Hill and the fate of their home hangs in the balance.

"Peter Donahue seems to have a map of old Seattle in his head … And all future attempts in its historical vein will be made in light of this book. "
David Guterson Author of *Snow Falling on Cedars*

Clown Girl Introduction by Chuck Palahniuk
Monica Drake
Fiction / 298pp / $15.95 / 0-9766311-5-6

Clown Girl lives in Baloneytown, a neighborhood so run-down that drugs, balloon animals, and even rubber chickens contribute to the local currency. Using clown life to illuminate a struggle between integrity and economic reality, this novel examines issues of class, gender, economics, and prejudice.

"The pace of [this] narrative is methamphetamine-frantic, as Drake drills down past the face paint and into Nita's core ... There is a lot more going on here than just clowning around."
Publishers Weekly

So Late, So Soon
D'Arcy Fallon
Memoir / 224pp / $15.95 / 0-9716915-3-3

An irreverent, fly-on-the-wall view of the Lighthouse Ranch, a Christian commune the eighteen-year-old hitchhiker D'Arcy Fallon called home for three years in the mid-1970s, when life's questions overwhelmed her and reconciling her family past with her future seemed impossible.

"What would draw an otherwise independent woman to a life of menial labor and subservience? Fallon's answer is both an inside look at '70s commune life and a funny, poignant coming of age."
Judy Blunt Author of *Breaking Clean*

September 11: West Coast Writers Approach Ground Zero Edited by Jeff Meyers
Essays / 266pp / $16.95 / 0-9716915-0-9

The events of September 11, 2001, their repercussions, and our varied responses to them inspired this collection. By history and geographic distance, the West Coast has developed a community different from the East; ultimately shared interests bridge the distinctions in provocative and heartening ways.

"*September 11: West Coast Writers Approach Ground Zero* deserves attention. This book has some highly thoughtful contributions that should be read with care on both coasts, and even in between."
San Francisco Chronicle

Dastgah: Diary of a Headtrip
Mark Mordue

Travel Memoir / 316pp / $15.95 / 0-9716915-6-8

A world trip that ranges from a Rolling Stones concert in Istanbul to meetings with mullahs and junkies in Teheran, from a cricket match in Calcutta to an S&M bar in New York, as Mark Morduc explores countries most Americans never see, as well as issues of world citizenship in the twenty-first century.

"Mordue has elevated *Dastgah* beyond the realms of the traditional travelogue by sharing not only what he learned about cultures he visited but also his brutally honest self-discoveries."
Elle

FINALIST, 2006 OREGON BOOK AWARD

The Cantor's Daughter
Scott Nadelson

Fiction / 280pp / $15.95 / 0-9766311-2-1

Sympathetic, heartbreaking, and funny, these stories – capturing people in critical moments of transition – reveal our fragile emotional bonds and the fears that often cause those bonds to falter or fail.

"These beautifully crafted stories are populated by Jewish suburbanites living in New Jersey, but ethnicity doesn't play too large a role here. Rather, it is the humanity of the characters and our empathy for them that bind us to their plights."
Austin Chronicle

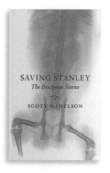

WINNER: 2004 OREGON BOOK AWARD;
2005 GLCA NEW WRITERS AWARD

Saving Stanley: The Brickman Stories
Scott Nadelson

Ficion / 230pp / $15.95 / 0-9716915-2-5

These interrelated short stories are graceful, vivid narratives that bring into sudden focus the spirit and the stubborn resilience of the Brickmans, a Jewish family of four living in suburban New Jersey. This fierce collection provides an unblinking examination of family life and the human instinct for attachment.

"Focusing on small decisions and subtle shifts, *Saving Stanley* closely examines the frayed ties that bind. With a fly-on-the-wall sensibility and a keen sense for dramatic restraint, Nadelson is ... both a promising writer and an apt documentarian."
Willamette Week

Seaview   Introduction by Robert Coover
Toby Olson
Fiction / 316pp / $15.95 / 0-9766311-6-4

This novel follows a golf hustler and his dying wife across an American wasteland. Trying to return the woman to her childhood home on Cape Cod, the pair are accompanied by a mysterious Pima Indian activist and shadowed by a vengeful drug dealer to the novel's apocalypse on the Seaview Links.

WINNER, 1983 PEN/FAULKNER AWARD

"Even a remarkable dreamer of nightmares like Nathanael West might have been hard-pressed to top the finale ... Unlike any other recent American novel in the freshness of its approach and vision."
The New York Times Book Review

The Well and the Mine
Gin Phillips
Fiction / $15.95 / 0-9766311-7-2

In 1931 Carbon Hill, Alabama, a small coal-mining town, nine-year-old Tess Moore watches a woman shove the cover off the family well and toss in a baby without a word. The apparent murder forces the family to face the darker side of their community and attempt to understand the motivations of their family and friends. Most townspeople don't have enough money for a newspaper and backbreaking work keeps them busy from dawn until well after dusk. But next to the daily toil of hard work are the lingering pleasures of sweet tea, feather beds, and lightning bugs.

Leaving Brooklyn   Introduction by Ursula Hegi
Lynne Sharon Schwartz
Fiction / 168pp / $12.95 / 0-9766311-4-8

An injury at birth left fifteen-year-old Audrey with a wandering eye and her own way of seeing; her relationship with a Manhattan eye doctor exposes her to the sexual rites of adulthood in this startling and wonderfully rich novel, which raises the themes of innocence and escape to transcendent heights.

"Stunning. Coming of age is seldom registered as disarmingly as it is in *Leaving Brooklyn*."
New York Times Book Review

Faraway Places Introduction by A.M. Homes
Tom Spanbauer
Fiction / $14.95 / 0-9766311-8-0

This novel marks the end of childhood for Jake Weber and the beginning of trouble for his family. An innocent swim ends with something far beyond anyone's expectations: Jake witnesses a brutal murder and is forced to keep quiet, even as the woman's lover is falsely accused.

"Forceful and moving ... Spanbauer tells his short, brutal story with delicacy and deep respect for place and character."
Publishers Weekly

FINALIST, 2005 OREGON BOOK AWARD

The Greening of Ben Brown
Michael Strelow
Fiction / 272pp / $15.95 / 0-9716915-8-4

Ben Brown becomes a citizen of East Leven, Oregon after he recovers from an electrocution that has turned him green. He befriends eighteen-year-old Andrew James and together they unearth a chemical-spill cover-up that forces the town to confront its demons and its citizens to choose sides.

"Strelow resonates as both poet and storyteller. [He] lovingly invokes ... a blend of fable, social realism, wry wisdom, and irreverence that brings to mind Ken Kesey, Tom Robbins, and the best elements of a low-key mystery."
The Oregonian

WINNER, 1987 PEN/FAULKNER AWARD

Soldiers in Hiding Introduced by Wole Soyinka
Richard Wiley
Fiction / 194pp / $14.95 / 0-9766311-3-X

Teddy Maki is a Japanese American jazz musician trapped in Tokyo with his friend, Jimmy Yakamoto, both of whom are drafted into the Japanese army after Pearl Harbor. Thirty years later, Maki is a big star on Japanese TV and wrestling with the guilt over Jimmy's death that he's been carrying since the war.

"Wonderful ... Original ... Terrific ... Haunting ... Reading *Soldiers in Hiding* is like watching a man on a high wire!"
The New York Times